THE HABIT OF A LIFETIME

By the Same Author

Cecil Chesterton
In the Dorian Mode: A Life of John Gray, 1866–1934
Like Black Swans: Some People and Themes
Olive Custance: Her Life and Work
Cancel All Our Vows: A Memoir of Joseph Gard'ner
My Dear Time's Waste
The Vatican Oracle
G.K.'s Weekly: An Appraisal
Footnote to the Nineties: A Memoir of John Gray and
    André Raffalovich
Saint Dominic's Press, 1919–1926: A Check-List of
    Printings and Publications
Three Private Presses

Edited by the same

Henry Williamson: the Man, the Writings
Frances Horovitz, Poet

Writing as Joseph Jerome

Montague Summers: A Memoir

THE HABIT OF A LIFETIME

BROCARD SEWELL

TABB HOUSE

First published 1992
Tabb House, 7 Church Street, Padstow, Cornwall, PL28 8BG

Typeset by Exe Valley Dataset Ltd, Exeter, Devon
Printed by Bookcraft, Midsomer Norton, Bath

Foreword

BENVENUTO CELLINI says that 'All men, whatever their condition, who have done anything of merit, or which really has a semblance of merit, if so be they are men of truth and good repute, should write the tale of their own life with their own hand.'

My Victorian relative William Sewell, Fellow of Exeter College, Oxon., would not have agreed. 'All biographies', he wrote, 'are in my own mind a delusion. They cannot and ought not to be true and faithful, because Truth and Faithfulness require that the whole man should be laid open to view, and Nature herself insists that this should not be done.' Nevertheless, William Sewell wrote his own *Reminiscences*: a thousand pages of them.

In justification he said that he had lived in a period of remarkable change, and had taken an active and not always a subordinate part in the controversies of the day, and that he had been brought into communication with many persons whose names have been prominent. Perhaps I can make a claim not too dissimilar. I have witnessed great and altogether unforeseen changes in the church, more especially in the life of the religious orders, with four of which I have been closely associated; so perhaps my recollections of how things were done *in diebus illis* may afford a grateful reminiscence of bygone days.

In the course of its writing, a book assumes a certain shape or pattern. In a book such as this some names and happenings that deserve to be included have inevitably had to be left out. Some that are omitted here are recorded in my diaries, and will also, I hope, be found at the last day recorded in the Book of Life.

BROCARD SEWELL

Contents

Acknowledgements

In the course of writing this book I have profited from conversations with Dom Edward Kelly, of the Canons Regular of the Lateran, and with Fr Bede Bailey, OP; I am much indebted also to Fr Patrick Fitzgerald-Lombard, O. Carm. for preparing the index, and to Brother Donald Halliday.

I am grateful to Saint Albert's Press for permission to incorporate, in revised form, passages from *My Dear Time's Waste*, a book of memoirs published, in a limited edition, in 1966. To Mrs Paul Silverthorne I am indebted for the title given to the present work, and for helpful criticisms of an earlier draft. And here it is right to remember my indebtedness to Caroline White, of Tabb House.

Thanks are due to Fr Conrad Pepler. Also to the Editor of *The Times* for permission to reprint letters from the Reverend Edward Kelly and myself which appeared in that newspaper.

For permission to make use of photographs by way of illustrations thanks are owing to Mr and Mrs K.L. Hughes, Mr Oswald Jones, Mr P.P. Thomas, and Sky Scan Balloon Photography; to the Rt Revd the Abbot of Nunraw for permission to reproduce the drawing by Peter F. Anson, and the Cornish Studies Library for the engraving of Dunheved (Launceston) Castle; and to Miss Jane Percival for her drawing.

BROCARD SEWELL

List of Illustrations

For

JANE PERCIVAL

CHAPTER ONE

A Cornish Childhood

Ah! native Cornwall! throned upon the hills,
Thy moorland pathways worn by Angel feet.
Thy streams that march in music to the sea
'Mid Ocean's merry noise, his billowy laugh!

R.S. Hawker, *The Quest of the Sangraal*

My early childhood was passed in Cornwall, and this I count
among the greatest blessings of my life. But I was not born there.
My birthplace was Bangkok, and the day was 30th July, 1912,
the feast day of Saints Abdon and Sennen, third-century Persian
martyrs, and the day of the Little Holiday celebrated annually by
the Muggletonians, followers of the Puritan sectary and prophet
Lodowick Muggleton. My father, Cecil Arthur Seymour Sewell,
at that time held a teaching post in the Royal Pages College,
Bangkok. In January 1912 he had married Ethel Dorothy Grylls,
elder daughter of Charles Reginald Gerveys Grylls, solicitor, of
Launceston, in Cornwall. Very soon after my birth my mother
succumbed to a tropical illness – there were no antibiotics then –
and I was sent back to England, in the care of a Thai *ayah*, to be
looked after by my grandparents.

I am not sure whether my earliest memories of place are of
Launceston or of Sutton Veney, in Wiltshire, where my other grandfather, Arthur Sewell, was the rector. Since my father could not
leave Bangkok, it was intended that I should live alternately with
my English and my Cornish grandparents; but the early death of
my grandmother at Sutton Veney resulted in my quite soon being
settled definitively in Launceston.

Before that, on 1st November, 1912, I was baptized by my

1

grandfather in the parish church of Sutton Veney, being there endowed with sacramental regeneration and the forenames Michael Gerveys Seymour: Michael after the Archangel, the patron saint of Cornwall; Gerveys after my uncle Gerveys Grylls; and Seymour after, I regret to say, Lord Protector Somerset, but more immediately after Marianne Billingsley Seymour, who had married Robert Burleigh Sewell, solicitor, my great-grandfather.

In 1912 my grandfather Arthur Sewell was seventy-one; but in my earliest memories of him he does not seem especially old. He was destined to reach his one hundred and fifth year, and retained all his faculties and remained reasonably active up to the end. A small, trim man, with silver hair and beard, his churchmanship was that of the Tractarians. That is to say, he believed in the apostolic succession, but in matters of liturgy he was low church, keeping strictly to the rubrics of the Book of Common Prayer. In celebrating the Holy Communion he never used vestments, but kept always to surplice, scarf, and the academic hood of an Oxford master of arts. In doctrine he was of a careful and exact orthodoxy. An exemplary pastor, he made the rounds of his parish by pony and trap; motor cars were still rare. To me he was always kind and affectionate, administering firm but gentle verbal reproof when this was required.

I think it must have been in 1916 that I moved from Sutton Veney to Launceston, and it was not until 1987 that I saw Sutton Veney again, for after he retired my grandfather settled in Salisbury, where I sometimes visited him. Here he seemed to live on little but tea and small fish-paste sandwiches, and occupied himself in writing a book in which he sought to vindicate the historical accuracy of all the events recorded in the Old Testament. Most unfortunately and unaccountably the manuscript of this work has been lost; it would have been interesting to see how he set about this quixotic task.

It was in 1987, while I was staying with my friend Jenny de Gex at Pilton, in Somerset, that we made an excursion by car to Sutton Veney, which was only an hour's run, if that. It was something like seventy years since I had last been there, and I should have been more prepared for changes than I was. The rectory and its garden, which I remembered as being very close to the church, had vanished. The notice board in the church porch disclosed that the parish no longer had a rector, but was cared for by a non-resident parson who had two or three other parishes to look after. This was sad; for if a village has no resident *curé* it may not actually be on the way to perdition but it is spiritually in a state of grave destitution.

But the greatest surprise was the church. I remembered it as having a steeple, but of its interior I remembered nothing. I had always thought of it as a venerable medieval fane; but it is in fact a modern church of the neo- Gothic order from the designs of the great John Loughborough Pearson, the architect of Truro Cathedral, Saint Augustine's, Kilburn, and other notable late Gothic Revival churches. The church at Sutton Veney is a very fine building, with elaborate Pearsonian interior decoration. It was a satisfaction to me to see my grandfather's name on the list of incumbents.

In the Loyal and Royal Borough of Launceston otherwise Dunheved I soon settled down with my other grandparents. This small, historic town, once the capital of Cornwall, stands on a hill just over the border from Devon, in the shadow of the massive circular keep of Dunheved Castle, built by Richard the First's brother the Earl of Mortain. Clearly visible from the Castle keep, to its east, lies Dartmoor; to the west is Bodmin Moor.

I believe that I had a very happy childhood in Launceston, but I cannot hope to recapture it for these pages. A child's memory and imagination usually emerge badly damaged after a boarding school education. But writers who can effectively recreate their childhood are rare; in many, if not most biographies the childhood chapters are the least effective. But let me do the best I can.

Trenuth, the house where I spent my early childhood, was the home of Charles Reginald Gerveys Grylls and his wife Ethel Chilcott, a Cornish lady 'of royal descent'. as the family tree is careful to note. The family of Grylls is one of the most ancient of Cornish families, claiming descent from a certain King Grylls of Marazion, who is mentioned in Kingsley's *Westward Ho!* Charles Grylls, my grandfather, was born in Helston, where his own branch of the extensive Grylls family had been prominent, as clergymen, lawyers, and bankers over the previous two hundred years. Oddly enough, these are the very professions which the Sewells had been following over the same period, principally in the Isle of Wight. Charles Grylls broke this long association with Helston when, soon after his marriage, he moved to Launceston and set up his own legal practice. He built himself a commodious new house, which he named Trenuth (The New Home) in Dunheved Road, a pleasant, leafy thoroughfare leading out of the town towards the Devon border. In those days a good proportion of what passed for 'society' in Launceston lived in Dunheved Road. Another large house, Manaton, belonged to the prominent Pethybridge family; the vicar, Canon Lewis, lived at Hendra, next door to Trenuth; a little further up, on the other side of the road, was our physician, Dr Gibson, and his family.

In those days, and for many years afterwards, the most influential people in Launceston were the Peter family, who owned the flourishing legal firm of Peter, Peter and Son, solicitors and commissioners for oaths. (I have often thought what fun it must be to be a commissioner for oaths; but the opportunity has never come my way.) The head of this family, old Mr Gerald Peter, as he was called to distinguish him from his son Gerald Peter the younger, lived in a very large house, Craigmore, which stood close to Windmill Hill, a high point beyond the eastern edge of the town. More recently established in the town was my grandfather's legal firm of Grylls and Cowlard.

In the sensational Charlotte Dymond murder trial at Bodmin in 1844 the solicitor for the prosecution, John Cowlard, was the father of my grandfather's partner H.L. Cowlard, while the solicitor for the defence, Richard Peter, was the father of old Mr Gerald Peter of Craigmore. And one of the three magistrates who heard the preliminary hearings was a member of the Chilcott family. This trial is the subject of Mrs Pat Munn's book *The Charlotte Dymond Murder*. which was successfully adapted for television some years ago. The trial at Bodmin, in which, it is hardly an exaggeration to say, nearly everyone concerned seems to have been related to all the other participants, issued in what now appears to have been a grave miscarriage of justice.

Nearly opposite my grandparents' house lived Stewart Peter, who had succeeded his father, old Mr Gerald Peter, as Town Clerk. Stewart's brother, Gerald the younger, lived with his family at The Bungalow, which was at the top of a steep, narrow drive. The back entrance to The Bungalow was just across the road from Craigmore. The two elder sons of young Mr Gerald Peter, Dick and Claud

Peter, were my special friends. Together we formed part of a small circle of children of the same social *milieu*; among them were the sons of the local veterinary surgeon, Mr Parsons, and of the manager of the town's principal bank, Mr Ogue.

I had more or less the *entrée* of The Bungalow and Craigmore. At Craigmore I used to play with Dick and Claud Peter, who were similarly welcome at Trenuth. At Craigmore we had more or less the run of the large gardens; but there were strict injunctions, which we were careful to observe, to keep off the flower beds. At tea-time of an afternoon Mrs Gerald Peter senior, a benign old lady dressed in Victorian black, would ply us with home-made chocolate cake. I am always hoping one day to come across chocolate cake of similar quality; so far I have been disappointed.

What games we played I do not remember; but I recall that at Trenuth we built a secret hideout behind a barrier of old man's beard, a rambling wild flower of the clematis family, on the roof of a toolshed in the garden. The pungent smell peculiar to pine trees always reminds me of Trenuth, where there were pine trees along the outer side of the drive. The drive has now vanished, and the pine trees too, so that the house, which has been divided into flats, is difficult to find.

Sometimes we went fishing, each with a jam-jar on a line, in the river Kensey, a tributary of the Tamar, which flows through Newport, the district, once a Rotten Borough, at the foot of the hill on which Launceston stands. Mostly we caught just minnows and tadpoles. Then we acquired bicycles; but it was not until a good deal later that I got up early one morning and cycled to Jamaica Inn, then a temperance house, and not yet made famous by Daphne Du Maurier's novel. From there I walked across Bodmin Moor and climbed Brown Willy, Cornwall's only mountain, from whose summit you can see the sea on either side of the peninsula.

Charles Grylls, my grandfather, was a tall, handsome man, with dark hair and moustache. I think I remember, but I cannot be sure, that he had some trace of Cornish accent. As I was to discover a good many years later, he seemed to find the bonds of matrimony straitening. My grandmother, Ethel Chilcott, took good care of me, helped by a nanny. She taught me to say my prayers, and to read, which I could do quite fluently at least by the time I was four. She used also to read aloud to me, from various works of piety and instruction: the Bible, of course, *Pilgrim's Progress*, and *Line Upon Line*; also from certain books intended for children: *The Fairchild Family*, *Holiday House*, and *Cast Up by the Sea*, an exciting tale by the explorer and hymn-writer Sir W.H. Baker.

When I was old enough my grandmother began to take me to church; but I do not think we went every Sunday. Saint Mary Magdalen's, the parish church of Launceston, was a good mile from Trenuth, and my grandfather owned neither horse and carriage nor a motor car. Presumably this economy enabled him to run Trenuth in suitable style, with a gardener, cook-general, and two maid-servants.

Apart from the usual small upsets of childhood my life at Trenuth was very happy. My grandparents were very good to me. I was fond of my nanny; our cook, Ivy Baker, allowed me to enter her fascinating subterranean domain: a great privilege this, I was given to understand. Pheasants were often to be seen hanging in the larder; usually they had been shot by my grandfather. Our two maids, who were sisters, handsome Cornish girls, must have been still in their teens. They waited at table, wearing black dresses and white capsand aprons. On Sundays the soup at luncheon appeared in a large silver tureen, preceding the traditional roast beef and Yorkshire pudding. I believe the Trenuth Yorkshire pudding was something special, a counterpart to the Craigmore chocolate cake. The horse-radish sauce that accompanied it was home-made, from plants in the garden. Our gardener, Mr Barrett, was another good friend. I believe that we boys gave him very little trouble.

When my nanny, or nursery governess left, as eventually she did, she was replaced more or less, but without being advanced to the style and dignity of the post, by one of our two maids. We often went for afternoon walks together; these sometimes took us to her home, on the further side of the railway tracks below the town. Ivy Baker's house was close by, and we sometimes called there. My grandparents undoubtedly knew of this, and approved. Their attitude was quite different from that of Mr Dombey when Susan Nipper took little Paul and Florence to her home in Staggs's Gardens, Camden Town.

Mr Barrett, our gardener, lived in a cottage about half way up Saint Stephen's Hill, on the further side of the Kensey valley, and almost opposite the Roman Catholic church of Blessed Cuthbert

Mayne and the English Martyrs. This small, domed granite Byzantine church is an architectural masterpiece, and it is a great pity that so few visitors to Launceston have it pointed out to them. It was built towards the end of the last century, when the Roman priest in the town was Canon Langdon, a native of the town who had formerly been a curate at Saint Mary Magdalen's. After his conversion and admission to the Catholic priesthood Father Langdon returned to Launceston, and adapted one of the rooms in the family home, which he had inherited, as a chapel for Catholic worship. His flock was small, but it increased, and in time this room-chapel was no longer large enough to accommodate the worshippers. The Canon had living with him, and on his bounty, an unsuccessful brother, a qualified architect who had done no work for years. One day, at breakfast, this brother said to the priest: "Arthur, you have been very good to me, and I have never done anything for you. I think I shall not be here much longer, and before I die I am going to design for you a really beautiful church." This he did, and in due time the church was built, and dedicated to Cuthbert Mayne, the first of the seminary priests from the Continent to die for his faith. He suffered at Launceston in the year 1577. The design and the furnishings and appointments of the church combined to make it a perfect shrine to the martyr's memory. Unhappily, an injudicious re-ordering of the sanctuary in the nineteen sixties has done much to destroy this effect. Although my *gouvernante* and I often passed this exotic-looking church, we never went inside it. I once asked what it was, and received no very clear answer.

One of the principal events in the Launceston calendar is the annual Cuthbert Mayne pilgrimage. On a Sunday in June each year the reliquary containing the martyr's skull is borne in procession from the church on Saint Stephen's hill to the Castle Green, where a commemorative service is held, and a sermon preached. The Bishop of Plymouth presides, and the Abbot of Buckfast and some of his monks are always present. Several hundred people, from all parts of the diocese of Plymouth, used to take part; but in recent years the attendance has fallen off, and the event has lost much of its splendour.

During my childhood I never so much as heard of this *manifestation*, as the French would say; it was as if in the town the pilgrimage was a taboo subject, except, of course, among the RCs. As I discovered many years later, 'upper class' Launceston thought this annual flaunting of 'Roman' religion to be in very bad taste. It had no very long history, and was the brainchild of a recent parish priest, Father Richard Alphonsus McElroy, who later was prior of the monastery of Canons Regular in Bodmin. In the late nineteen thirties, by which time I had become a Catholic myself, when I was revisiting Launceston, a prominent resident of the town said to me, apropos of the pilgrimage: "I cannot think why McElroy does it." (Father McElroy was well known, and respected throughout the length and breadth of Cornwall. His too early death in 1940, just when it was expected that his appointment as Abbot would be announced, was a sad blow to the cause of religion in Cornwall.)

At Trenuth my grandmother was careful to teach me good manners and the elements of social behaviour. My impression is that I was somewhat spoiled by my grandparents, and by my aunt Phyllis Grylls, my mother's younger sister, a very attractive young woman who was then still living at home. However, I did experience one major upset, and it taught me a lesson. The drawing room at Trenuth was a light and airy apartment, with chintz furniture-coverings; it was very much my grandmother's domain. A door from the drawing-room led into the conservatory, which was very much my grandfather's territory, although it was actually tended by Mr Barrett, the gardener. It was deliciously warm all the year round, for it was heated by hot-water pipes in the winter, and was filled with pots of sweet-smelling begonias, gloxinias, geraniums, and other plants.

Some days before my birthday one year, when I was perhaps five or six, I was nosing around in the conservatory when I noticed on a shelf the biggest and glossiest apple I had ever seen. I looked at it in astonishment, and picked it up. The temptation to eat it there and then was overwhelming; but I hesitated. It was not, my conscience reminded me, *my* apple. But surely to take a tiny nibble could do no harm? A second or so later it was done. The bite was of the smallest, scarcely visible. But I knew I had done wrong. Turning the apple round, so as to conceal the bite – perhaps if someone noticed it they would think a mouse had done it? – I replaced it on the shelf.

For some days nothing happened. Then, one morning, my

grandfather asked me if I had touched a large apple in the conservatory? I could not deny it. My grandfather then said: "What a pity. That apple was meant for you on your birthday." There were no further reproaches, and no punishment.

Of the 1914-1918 war I have only vague memories. I remember seeing a military airship hovering over the town square; and I remember looking at the bulletins of war news that were posted up outside Brimmell's stationer's shop. On Armistice Day, 11th November, 1918, I hung out a Siamese flag, red, with a white elephant in the centre, from my bedroom window.

Even in wartime, parties were a feature of Launceston's juvenile society. I remember meeting Dick Peter one day, this must have been in 1919, when we were both out with our nannies, and his greeting me with the question: "When is that party of yours coming off?" To which I gravely replied: "It's hanging fire – like the Peace Conference." Which seems to indicate an early interest in public affairs.

I remember a children's Christmas party, with dancing, held at Eagle House, in Castle Street. This Georgian mansion is perhaps the finest house in Launceston. It belonged then to the parents of a little girl called Lettice Birch. Today it is an hotel.

At an early age, three perhaps, I began to attend a kindergarten school in a house at the bottom of the drive leading up to The Bungalow. Dick and Claud Peter also were among the pupils. But when the lady who ran it migrated to British Columbia we were old enough to transfer to Pendruccombe, a private high school for girls which admitted a few boys up to the age of ten or so. There were thirty or forty pupils, some of them boarders. Pendruccombe was in the Tavistock road, on the other side of the town from Trenuth; but it could be reached by turning left at the crossroads at the top of Dunheved Road. It was too far for me to walk if I was to be there by the required time, 9 a.m. How the Peter boys got there I do not remember; I had the pleasure of going on horseback, riding pillion behind one of Dr Gibson's daughters, who had a horse of her own. Here was no creeping like snail unwillingly to school. In fact, Pendruccombe is the one educational establishment of which I have only pleasant memories.

This small school really did instil into the very young the rudiments of learning and culture. Pendruccombe was a large red brick house, with a big garden, in which my companion's horse could graze at its ease until it was time for us to go home. The school was owned and run by two maiden ladies, sisters, the Misses Seccombe, who were certainly well educated, but had, so far as I know, no formal academic qualifications. They had something better: a great love and appreciation of our English cultural heritage, and the happy art of gently immersing children in it in the most agreeable way possible. The two ladies were known in the school as Miss Leo and Miss Minnie respectively. Miss Leo, the elder, was small, slightly plump, white-haired, and of a simple, natural dignity. Her sister was thinner, grey-haired, and more vivacious, a connoisseur of the novels and stories of W.W. Jacobs, her favourite reading, to which she introduced us.

Their principal assistant, Miss Caird, whose first name appeared to be a closely guarded secret, was a handsome young Scotswoman with red hair. She was a graduate, and wore an academic gown in the classroom. Miss Caird was an excellent teacher. Dick and Claud Peter and myself were only six or seven when she started us off in French and Latin, in which we made good progress under her instruction.

The educational standard at Pendruccombe was good. I do not remember who taught us arithmetic, but whoever it was had no success with me; but I should think my incapacity was probably inborn. Pendruccombe was a happy school, and I have no recollection of punishments or other disagreeablenesses. Memories of my fellow-pupils have mostly faded, but one could hardly not remember the two beautiful teenage Gibson sisters. I remember also a small boy called Justin Hull, and a little girl whose name eludes me who was a grand-daughter of the Reverend Sabine Baring-Gould, novelist, folklorist, and hymn writer, who held the living of Lew Trenchard, in Devon, only a few miles away.

I think I was singularly blessed to have been so happy both at home and at school in those early years. Trenuth was a hospitable house. My grandfather's chief cronies were Alderman Trood and Major Soper, the latter being the manager of a local brickworks. Thomas Pomeroy Trood, a former mayor of Launceston, was a short, stocky man, Alderman Grylls was tall and well proportioned. Seen together in photographs they remind one irresistibly of Colonel Up and Mr Down. Mr Trood once distinguished himself as the town's chief magistrate by quashing the case against a certain delinquent whom everyone expected to see consigned to the stocks, if not transported to Botany Bay, so to speak. Mayor Trood gave his reasons for discharging the offender in a judgement which sent gales of laughter through the court-room; but alas there seems to be no record of Mayor Trood's Great Judgement. Today there seems to be no one in Launceston who can remember it.

Another great friend of my grandfather's, who often came to stay at Trenuth, was Max Schiller (Mr F.P.M. Schiller, KC), who was a brother of the German-born Cambridge philosopher F.C.S. Schiller. Max Schiller was my grandfather's favourite companion on shooting and fishing excursions. It seems that I was to have been named after him, for one of my christening presents was a Book of Common Prayer given to me by my great-aunt Emily Grylls, and inscribed by her 'To Max'. I do not know why the name was dropped, but I am not sorry to have escaped it. I have good memories of Mr Schiller, who in later years helped me out of a serious financial difficulty. His family was Jewish; I do not know how or why he and his brother came to be settled in England, long before the National Socialist régime came to power in Germany.

A curious thing about my life at Trenuth, though it struck no one as unusual at the time, was that I was never taken to have my hair cut: Frankie Mules, the barber, always came to Trenuth to perform this rite. Mr Mules owned a flourishing tobacconist's and barber's shop in The Square. On market days he cut the hair of farmers from miles around; and his wife, an amiable lady, dispensed to them, in one form or another, large quantities of tobacco. Some years later, after my grandfather had retired, Frankie Mules bought the quite large house which had formerly been the offices of Messrs Grylls and Cowlard, and converted it into a desirable residence for himself and his wife. It was said at the time that if he had wanted to he could have papered its walls with five-pound notes. I daresay he could.

Charles Grylls's legal practice necessitated his making quite frequent business trips all over Cornwall. He had no car; presumably because, although he passed for a man of substance, his income was not quite equal to it on top of running Trenuth in what he considered an appropriate style. So on these business excursions he was usually driven by his friend Major Soper, who owned a Hupmobile motor car, an American vehicle then popular in England. Clearly the Major enjoyed these days off from the brickworks, and was happy to act as chauffeur. It was on one of these outings, when I was perhaps six or seven, that I had my first alcoholic drink: sherry and bitters, then a favourite aperitif, in the Headland Hotel at Newquay. Newquay was the first seaside resort I stayed at. Each summer my great-aunt Emmie Grylls, who lived in Truro, took me either to Newquay or to Bude for a short holiday. In those days Newquay was a quiet place, where one of the mild excitements available to visitors was watching the lifeboat and its crew making their practice launch down a slipway on the cliff into the sea. This must still be a sight worth seeing, even though the chute does not seem to me today as long and as steep as it did in my childhood.

From time to time I went to stay with my godfather, the Reverend Joseph Gunning, who had been a close friend of my mother's. Mr Gunning was the vicar of Saint Erme, near Probus, and was later vicar of Saint Mawgan, in the Vale of Lanherne. Mr and Mrs Gunning had three children, Joy, Betty, and John, with whom I could play in the large vicarage garden; but I can remember nothing of our games apart from one which had something to do with our belief in fairies, and involved the attempt to find a four-leafed clover, which would have enabled us to see these little beings.

The vicarage at Saint Mawgan was a very large house – today the parson lives in a much smaller one – standing on high ground on the opposite side of the vale from the church. From the vicarage a walk of twenty minutes or so brought you to the sea at Mawgan Porth. Here we used to bathe, from a beach that we often had more or less to ourselves. Today it is less secluded, and is overlooked by an hotel of the concrete and cement kind, and is disfigured by a rash of caravans on a nearby site.

Later Mr Gunning was made a canon of Truro Cathedral. He died in 1947, and is still remembered affectionately by the older people in Saint Mawgan. He was a devoted parish priest, of broad Catholic churchmanship; towards the end of his life he was troubled by a sense of failure in his ministry. His parishioners, both at Saint Erme and Saint Mawgan, would not have agreed.

Next to the church at Saint Mawgan, separated from it only by a hedge with a gap in it, is the Carmelite convent of Lanherne, a house which dates from Saxon times and has always been faithful to the Old Religion. One night during the nineteen thirties the convent caught fire. Long before the fire brigade arrived Mr Gunning was up on the roof, fighting the flames. For this act he was publicly thanked by the Bishop of Plymouth, Dr Barrett, who a little later took him inside the nuns' enclosure so that they might thank him personally. Mr Gunning was very proud of having been accorded this rare privilege.

My father did not return to England until eight years after my mother's death. Early in 1920 my grandparents heard that he would be coming home on leave in the summer. The day came, and in the afternoon we walked down the hill to meet him at the station. I have no recollection of his actual arrival, nor of our return up the hill. It was a hot summer day; I doubt if we would have asked a tired traveller from London to face a walk up the very steep road from the station to the town, or the even steeper short cut known as The Zigzag, a narrow defile with a notice at either end warning the wayfarer of danger from falling rocks. Perhaps we got a lift as far as The Square in a horse-drawn cab belonging to one or other of the town's two principal hotels. From that point we would have walked the rest of the way to Trenuth.

A week or two later my father took me to join my uncle Humphry Grylls and his wife Gladys in a seaside holiday at Portscatho, a fishing village near Falmouth, which at that time was not yet the popular holiday resort that it became later. There were not many other visitors there. The sun shone, and we spent a good part of each day on the beach, where we made friends with a Dr and Mrs Coldstream, from London, who were on holiday with their three daughters and their son William, who was only two or three years older than myself. My father, a reasonably young and good-looking man for his thirty-nine years, fell in love with the youngest Coldstream girl, Nancy, who was nineteen, and soon they were engaged. We all liked the Coldstream family; the holiday was considered to have been a great success. This holiday was, in fact, the final episode of my Cornish childhood, 'Life's morning hour', to borrow a phrase from the writer E.H. Visiak, who I suspect may have borrowed it from someone else: possibly Milton?

Since my ordination in 1954 I have been able during most years to return to Cornwall for a week or two. This has been made possible largely through the generous hospitality of Colin and Joy Wilson at Gorran Haven. Joy Wilson has become, through her energetic fieldwork, an authority on Cornish history and topography, and has published some well researched and illustrated studies of Old Saint Austell, Old Mevagissey, and the area generally. I have had many enjoyable excursions with her to out-of-the-way places, such as Golden, near Probus, the manor where Saint Cuthbert Mayne was arrested, and Court Farm (formerly Court Manor) at Lanreath, where the Grylls of Helston family has its Cornish origins.

Colin Wilson has at least twenty thousand books in his house, and has read every one of them. What is more, he has understood them, and can remember their contents. And if he has not yet written twenty thousand books it is not for want of trying. His energy and dedication to work are remarkable. He is rarely seen until 4 o'clock or so in the afternoon when he surfaces from his subterranean study, to take his two Saint Bernard dogs for a walk on the cliffs. Then follows the evening meal by the fire – even on a summer evening a fire is appropriate in Cornwall – with talk, music, or television if there is anything interesting to be seen. And so to bed. He does not keep late hours.

The poet and novelist Penelope Shuttle and her husband Peter Redgrove, and their daughter Zoe, live in Falmouth, and a meeting with them is part of my yearly Cornish programme.

CHAPTER TWO

Warfare of a Public School

AT the end of the summer term in 1920 I left Pendruccombe, sentenced to enter in September the Junior School at Cheltenham College. This was Charles Grylls's old school, and I think my uncles Glynn and Humphry Grylls had been there too. Sending me to Cheltenham must certainly have been my grandfather's idea, and it was not a good one, though well-intended. Dunheved College, five minutes' walk from Trenuth, was an excellent school; but it was then considered necessary that the sons of upper middle class parents should receive a 'public school' education, preferably as a boarder.

Before I went to Cheltenham my father took me on a visit to London, where we stayed at the Russell Hotel. Nancy Coldstream, my father's fiancée, who was with her parents in Brondesbury, joined us every day. She was a bright, attractive girl, and I liked her very well. While we were in London I was taken, as part of my entertainment, or education perhaps?, to see two popular musical comedies that were then playing: *Chu Chin Chow* and *The Maid of the Mountains*. This seems to me an odd choice of amusement for a child of barely eight; but perhaps there was nothing more suitable available. I certainly did not enjoy these two long-running shows as much as I had enjoyed the pantomime *Little Red Riding Hood* as presented one Christmas in the Town Hall at Launceston.

At the Russell Hotel the Australian singer Dorothy Helmrich, who was staying there at the time, was very kind to me. I remember trailing through the hotel's rooms and corridors a large yellow wooden crocodile on a string, which opened and shut its jaws with a clacking sound. My father and my young stepmother were soon to sail for Bangkok, and would not be in England again for several

15

years. I was not present at their wedding, and do not know where it took place.

Objectively considered, to remove a small boy suddenly from the only home he had ever known, and which he loved, and to plant him down among strangers in the totally alien milieu of a unisex boarding school, must be considered an act of cruelty. But it was not meant as such. Like other parents and guardians I am sure that my father and grandfather believed that by doing this they were securing for me, at no small expense, a highly privileged position. What they achieved in fact was my reduction to a state of bewildered disorientation. However, life in the Junior School at Cheltenham was in some ways not so bad once you got used to it. On Sundays all the boys, both in the Junior and Senior Schools, wore Eton suits and collars, to which we added, when out walking in the afternoon, mortar boards (academic caps) with red tassels. One can readily imagine what derision such attire would excite today!

In my disorientation I did not take to preparatory school life; I was soon in trouble for various kinds of misbehaviour, and made scant progress in my studies. Nevertheless, it was at Cheltenham that I received the only prize I have ever won in my life. It was not awarded for any specific scholastic achievement, but for something supplementary; hardly good conduct, but general knowledge perhaps. I received this prize on the school's speech day from the hands of Lord Lee of Fareham, a prominent Old Cheltonian: a copy of Kipling's book of stories, *The Day's Work*, bound in red leather, with the school's coat of arms embossed in gold on the front cover. I kept the book for a good many years, but I never enjoyed its contents, and eventually it got lost. The best thing in it, to my mind, was a printed Latin certificate of merit pasted inside the front cover, and signed by the Headmaster of Cheltenham, H.H. Hardy.

After a year of receiving uniformly bad reports about me from 'Old Thorny' (Mr Thornton, the headmaster of the Junior School, a good disciplinarian, and a kind and likeable man) my father became dissatisfied, and decided to transfer me to his own old school, Weymouth College, whose Junior School I entered in the summer of 1922. Founded in 1862 it was a minor public school run on low church lines by a charitable trust registered as Evangelical

Church Schools Limited. In the course of its existence – financial difficulties brought it to an end in 1940 – the school produced a number of distinguished men. Its alumni tended to become low church clergymen, colonial bishops, officers in the Armed Forces, and settlers and administrators of the far-flung British Empire. Among its more distinguished alumni were the ill-fated Liberal politician and cabinet minister C.F.G. Masterman, Stuart Hibbard of the BBC, Flight-Lieutenant Stainforth, the Schneider Trophy winner, Father Stephen Bedale, sometime superior of the Society of the Sacred Mission (no low churchman he), Vice-Admiral Sir Ronald Brockman, KCB (still happily with us), and my late uncle, Robert Beresford Sewell, FRS, marine biologist.

Weymouth College – it still retains the name – is in the Dorchester Road, a little way out of the town. After its closure as a public school in 1940 it was for some time a Teachers' Training College. Today, in 1991, it is what is called a Tertiary College; that is, a sixth form college within the 'Comprehensive' system. Its main building by Crickmay, a local architect who at one time employed Thomas Hardy, has a certain dignity, but is not exactly architecturally impressive. It stands a little way back, on the right hand side of the road as it leaves the town; beside it, to the right, is the former chapel, now a library, a neat building with faintly Gothic features. Behind the chapel is a block of old farm buildings known as Nangles, which had been converted into science laboratories.

Beyond these buildings was a big corrugated iron gymnasium, the fives courts, and an open space where the Officers' Training Corps was drilled. Beyond these again was the cricket field, which was said to be the finest in the south of England. This field, which was big enough to allow of three or four games of cricket going on at the same time, is now covered with the residences and offices of the Tertiary College. At some little distance from the cricket field, and on very rough ground, were the rugby football pitches. Many a tedious afternoon have I spent there, unwillingly, often in pouring rain, taking part in this violent and dangerous game.

Scarcely less tedious than 'rugger' was cricket, in the summer months. My family were supposed to be great cricketers. Certainly my father and grandfather were devotees of King Willow. I never took to the game; but it had a certain lazy charm of a warm summer afternoon. At least when faced with the boredom of 'fielding' –

welcome relief though that was from the perils of the wicket – one could enjoy the magnificent view over Weymouth Bay as far as Saint Aldhelm's Head away to the east. In those days Weymouth was advertized on the posters of the Great Western Railway as 'The Naples of England'. This perhaps was a little far-fetched; but still, Weymouth was and is an attractive place. It was a favourite watering-place of King George the Third. The fine red-brick mansion where he used to stay now fronts the sea as the Gloucester Hotel.

Sometimes our day-boys' parents would come to watch our cricket; conversation with them could be interesting and amusing. For instance, Weymouth's chief customs and excise officer, Mr Brambleby, who wore a blazer and straw hat, and smoked a pipe, liked to discourse about the descent which he claimed from one Doeg the Edomite: cf. I Samuel xxi, 7: 'And his name was Doeg the Edomite, the chiefest of the herdsmen that belonged to Saul.'

The Junior School was situated in the Dorchester Road, immediately facing the main building of the College. In 1922 the headmaster of the College was Robert Russ Conway, MA, sometime scholar of Saint Catherine's College, Cambridge, where he had been contemporary with my father. The head of the Junior School was one E.C.H. Moule, Esq., who was guardedly described in the school's prospectus as 'late of Ridley Hall, Cambridge'.

Moule, who was known to the boys under his care as 'Uncle Ernest', was an unusual personality, and not altogether a likeable one. He had left the University without taking his degree, and was surmised by the more inquiring among his pupils to be in some undefined way the black sheep of his distinguished Dorset family. He had spent a good many years as a schoolmaster in Japan, where he had become a champion at ju-jitsu, or judo as we would say today. Uncle Ernest was a tall, rather heavily-built man. He dressed in sober suitings of near-clerical grey, often worn together with an Eton collar and bow tie: a bizarre attire, but it seemed to become him. His manner was suavity itself, an impressive exhibition of old-world courtesy; but he had a formidable gift of sarcasm, with which he used to quell boys, staff, and parents alike. He was to some degree feared by those under his authority. His wife, Josephine, a sister of the bishop of Winchester, Dr Woods, was a gentle lady, well liked by the boys. Mr and Mrs Conway, whom he was unable to bully, derived endless entertainment from Uncle Ernest's vagaries; but it is safe to say that he would never have been their choice as headmaster of the Junior School. It is hard to imagine how he got the job; but boards of governors can be susceptible to charm, of which Ernest Moule could mount an impressive display when he wanted to.

His nerve was astounding. When on duty he always wore a Cambridge MA gown, and carried a mortar board academic cap. To see him sweep into the chapel and up the aisle on Sunday morning thus attired was to receive a lesson in deportment worthy of Mr Turveydrop. Not many non-graduates, I fancy, would care to put on such a display as this, and seat themselves in a back row of choirstalls alongside robed Masters and Bachelors, and a silk-gowned and scarlet-hooded Cambridge Doctor of Letters (Uncle Ernest's brother, H.F. Moule).

Uncle Ernest's gown when not in use hung on a peg in one of the Junior School corridors. One day, when no one was about, I ventured to examine it, and was not altogether surprised to find sewn inside it a cloth label bearing the name of his other brother, Archdeacon Moule, the vicar of Abbotsbury.

There seems to have been a touch of sadism in Ernest Moule; he frequently administered canings to troublesome small boys. Perhaps there was nothing very unusual about this at that time; but supposed major offenders were punished by a public ritual caning, carried out in one of the classrooms, in the presence of all the boys and the staff. I myself received one of these ritual chastisements, for a not very grave offence that had not actually been committed, but only contemplated. The Matron had been eavesdropping, and made a report.

When administering corporal punishment Uncle Ernest never exceeded the six strokes of the cane that were the customary maximum; and he never went too far with his lashes, at least by the standards of those times. He had his merits. He inspired in us a love of reading, and, through his Sunday evening gramophone recitals, of music. He taught us, if we needed teaching, good manners. His impressive old-world courtesy worked wonders with parents and prospective parents, of pupils. His polished flights of sarcasm could be very entertaining: as long as you were not their recipient. One of his favourite butts was Eric Le Mesurier, a timid, bespectacled boy of rather 'old-ladyish' appearance. I remember Uncle Ernest shouting out to him when he was performing rather badly as a batsman in a game of cricket: "Why not try using your umbrella, Le Mesurier?" A quip that vastly amused the bystanders, but not at all him at whom it was aimed. Wing-Commander LeMesurier (as he became) was killed on active service as a fighter pilot in 1943, which shows us that physical frailty or sensitivity is no bar to courage.

At the Junior School there was always some young unqualified usher in residence as second master. Some of these did not stay long. One, an active member of the British Fascisti – a pre-Mosley movement of short duration – got himself involved with a servant girl at Pennsylvania Castle, on the Isle of Portland, the home of three brothers who were boarders at the school, and had to migrate speedily to Australia. He was a likeable man, and we missed him. Another young usher got undesirably mixed up with some of the boys, and he also quickly vanished. He was replaced by a hefty, red-haired young man named Kennedy, some kind of relative, so we understood, of Uncle Ernest. Kennedy was over six feet in height, and was a considerable athlete.

One day Uncle Ernest announced that he would shortly put on, during school hours, a ju-jitsu demonstration, to be held in the gymnasium, a wooden hut at the bottom of the garden. We all looked forward to this. Ernest Moule was not a boastful man, but somehow it was understood in the school that he was the equal of Japan's foremost ju-jitsu wrestlers.

On the appointed morning the whole school, pupils and staff, assembled in the gym, where mattresses had been put down in the middle of the floor. Uncle Ernest and Mr Kennedy duly appeared, wearing white cricket shirts and white flannel trousers, and gym shoes, ready for the fray. In spite of the difference in their ages – Kennedy was about twenty, Moule perhaps forty – they seemed physically well matched. Uncle Ernest's weight might have been a bit of a handicap for him; on the other hand, Kennedy's knowledge of ju-jitsu was nil.

When all was ready, Uncle Ernest announced: "Now boys, we ju-jitsu wrestlers can throw any assailant, however strong. Mr Kennedy is a much younger man than I, but he will be quite unable to put me on the ground." Then, turning to his opponent, who stood at three or four yards' distance from him: "Now, Mr Kennedy, I want you to come at me with all your strength. Don't be afraid of hurting me. Use all the force you can. NOW!"

There stood Uncle Ernest in a posture of confident self-defence. And there was Kennedy, charging at him with all his might. In a second or two it was all over. Uncle Ernest lay prostrate and groaning on the floor, unable to rise. An arm had been broken in his fall. Like all the ranks of Tuscany – Uncle Ernest himself had introduced us to Lord Macaulay's famous poem – we could scarce forebear to cheer. But forebear we did: the shock was too great. Which was as well for us; any applause would have had to be paid for dearly later on.

While I was at the Junior School there occurred a curious instance of what would seem to have been collective hallucination. A number of us, perhaps half a dozen or so, were laid up with measles, and were segregated in a long dormitory. My bed was at one end of the room, with a wall behind it; the other boys were in beds to the left and right of a central aisle. In the middle of one night we were all awake; I think a thunderstorm was the cause. We were talking quietly among ourselves when I suddenly exclaimed: "Look at those two black men." At the further end of the dormitory I could see two black men. who began to walk, side by side, down the length of the room, between the two rows of beds, and then vanished into the wall beside my bed. Everyone in the room saw them, and very distinctly.

My grandmother Ethel Grylls had died in 1919; not long afterwards Charles Grylls married again. His second wife was Agnes Townend, the daughter of a clergyman, and one of my grandfather's old flames. I took the death of my much loved grandmother hard, and was intensely resentful of her successor. I behaved very badly towards her; so much so that there could be no question of my remaining under her care. In any case, Alderman Grylls had decided to sell Trenuth, which was certainly much too big for just two people; he and the second Mrs Grylls moved to The White Hart hotel, in The Square, where they were very comfortable.

As a temporary measure I was farmed out during the school holidays from Cheltenham to a lady who took in waifs and strays of different kinds at her cottage in a Herefordshire village. This lady had been recommended to my father by one of the canons of

Hereford Cathedral. She did her best for me, I do not doubt; but the arrangement was an uneasy one. Happily for me, after I had moved from Cheltenham to Weymouth it was arranged that I should spend my holidays with the Coldstream family in London at Number Ten, Garlinge Road, Brondesbury, towards the top of the Edgware Road. George and Lilian Coldstream, my step-grandparents, were as kind to me as Charles and Ethel Grylls had been, and their unmarried daughter, Winnie, was no less so. Her brother William, the future knight, was not much older than I, and we got on well together. Bill Coldstream was already beginning to paint pictures, of which he gave me one, but the great distinction that he was to achieve as a painter was not yet suspected. We shared a common interest in zoology, and together we formed a collection of tortoises, terrapins, grass-snakes, Japanese tree-frogs, and other small creatures, which we bought at Messrs Derry and Toms's store in Kensington High Street. Bill Coldstream had an inventive mind and was a great story-teller, which talent I did my best to rival. In the attic bedroom that we shared we created an entire fictional kingdom, the doings of whose monarch and his subjects were elaborated in a seemingly endless serial story.

During the school holidays I went a good deal to the cinema, mostly to the Blue Hall, near the Marble Arch end of the Edgware Road. There was nothing 'blue' about the films shown there; among them were such fine pictures as *The Moon of Israel*, *Orphans of the Storm*, about the French Revolution, with Lilian Gish as its star, if I remember correctly, *The Four Horsemen of the Apocalypse*, with Rudolph Valentino, and *Captain Blood*, an early Errol Flynn picture, from the novel by Rafael Sabatini. Somewhere, but not at the Blue Hall, I saw that masterpiece of the macabre *The Cabinet of Dr Caligari*, rivalled for sinister effect only by *Nosferatu*, which I saw much later, at a private showing in 1981. These were all silent films, musical accompaniment and 'effects' being usually supplied by a trio or quartet of musicians. (The first film that I ever saw was part of a serial of *The Pickwick Papers*, shown in the old cinema in a back street of Launceston, where the musical accompaniment was provided by a pianist, solo. That must have been about 1917 or 1918.)

But now, in the late nineteen twenties, the 'talkies' were about to arrive. My first experience of them, in 1926 or 1927, was at the

Tivoli Cinema – long since, like the Blue Hall, demolished – in the Strand, close to Charing Cross station. The double bill featured an episode from *Bleak House*, with Bransby Williams as Grandfather Smallweed; this was followed by a picture in which the American comedians Wheeler and Woolsey were shown struggling to get a grand piano into an apartment whose door was too small to admit it.

In those days an exciting adventure was to ride down the Edgware Road on the upper deck of a bus. The red buses of the London General Omnibus Company had a number of rivals, of various colours. All these buses had open upper decks, whose seats were each provided with a tarpaulin as some small protection against rain. Competition between the buses of the various companies was keen; the principal rivals and competitors of the red General buses were those of the dark blue Admiral line. From Cricklewood to the Marble Arch the Edgware Road runs very slightly downhill; the General and Admiral buses used to race each other, at quite frightening speeds. The sedate pace of today's London buses would have been regarded as cowardly; the era of semi- permanent traffic jams had not yet arrived.

But to return to Weymouth: in the autumn of 1925, at the age of thirteen, I crossed the Dorchester road and entered Weymouth College proper, the Senior School. I had been allocated to the Headmaster's house, the school's main building, where most of the one hundred or so boarders lived. Rumours about what went on in the Senior School were always rife among the juniors, and some of the rumours were disturbing. However, the transition proved quite easy. Bullying was not unknown in the Senior School, but it did not come my way. Which is strange, for I was an entirely unathletic boy, with no interest in or aptitude for sport or games of any kind. Nor did I belong to the OTC (Officers' Training Corps); not because of any pacifist inclinations, but simply because 'the Corps' was an extra on the school bill, and my father could not afford it. Moreover, although lazy at my studies, I was unmistakably some kind of 'swot', fond of reading and so on. All this might well have made me a prime candidate for victimization; but in fact it brought me no such unpleasant experiences.

The horarium or daily programme began with a compulsory early morning plunge into a bath of cold water. This – though of course it was not explained to us – was supposed to damp down or inhibit our burgeoning sexuality. I doubt if it had much success in that direction. This disagreeable exercise one dodged if one could, which was not often. Compulsory games, on three afternoons each week, there was no avoiding, unless one were genuinely unwell or partially disabled. Other trials were the lack of privacy, the tiresome PT (physical training), and the aridity of the low church public school religion as purveyed in the chapel. But at the time I was not really conscious of the unnaturalness of the unisex régime, under which the only women one saw were mostly servants.

'Fagging', that is to say, acting as servants at the beck and call of the prefects – senior boys entrusted with a certain degree of authority for the maintenance of order and discipline – I did not find especially burdensome, and one quite soon passed beyond it. But one went in some awe of the prefects, for they were authorised to punish offenders against good order. For instance, they could beat you in your pyjamas with the hard sole of felt slipper: a punishment feared as much as, if not more than, a caning by the headmaster.

In 1923 Mr Conway was nearing retirement. He was a stockily built man, of medium height, with grey hair and moustache, and a limp, the result of some athletic injury of long ago. He was a good classical scholar and an effective teacher and disciplinarian. Fair and just in his judgements, he was not to be trifled with. His manner was at once brusque and genial. In the school he was respected and well liked. His wife, Bertha, was a small woman with a marked sense of humour. She was active in the life of the school, supervising the commissariat and other domestic arrangements. In the chapel on Sundays she presided at the organ, and her lively voluntaries before and after the service had something of a virtuoso touch. Her range of intellectual sympathies was perhaps a little narrow. Leanings towards Roman Catholicism, for instance, she could not approve; but she could make jokes about the Pope and his adherents that were funny without being offensive. By the time a boy came to leave Weymouth College, if not before, he had usually discovered that Mr and Mrs Conway were friends who could be trusted and relied on for life.

The Second Master, H.W. Major, was the senior mathematics teacher; there were no heads of departments in those days, and I fancy schools were better off without them. Major was a large, heavy man, of Chestertonian proportions, strongly resembling – in part because of his moustache – the film actor and comedian Oliver Hardy. In the school Major was known to the boys as Gobi; perhaps, for he also taught geography, from a catch-phrase of his: 'The Gobi desert is a great waste', a statement that always caused much mirth in the classroom. He was reputed once to have been a mathematician of exceptional brilliance, and an outstanding athlete. His classes were apt to be entertaining, but one did not learn a great deal from them. He enjoyed a joke, and had a fund of good stories. His usual way of beginning a class was to ask: "What were we doing last day?" When informed, he would as often as not go through once again all that he had said on the previous occasion.

In the classroom Gobi was inclined to be easygoing. He did not keep order very effectively, but he never allowed things to get too much out of hand. I remember a geography class when he gave us a vivid account of the re-laying in one night of the Great Western Railway's line between London and Bristol, when the change was made from the broad gauge to the narrow. In actual fact, this operation was performed in one week; a sufficiently remarkable achievement, but evidently not remarkable enough for Mr Major. I do not really think that I ever learned anything from him at all; but I am sure that was as much my fault as his.

My best subject was English, though I did well in Latin, French, and History. Rather less well in Greek, but sufficiently so. We were fortunate in having a teacher of English language and literature of rare brilliance, Lionel Gough, an Oxford graduate who later taught at Haileybury, Marlborough, and Downside. Gough, whose father was vicar of Tewkesbury, was a keen Anglo- Catholic. This fact he had to keep rather quiet at so low church a school as Weymouth; but he was willing enough to talk about matters of religion in the privacy of his study to anyone who was interested.

Modern languages (French, German and Spanish) were taught by a middle-aged Scots lady, Miss Roberts, who had come to the school during the 1914-1918 war, when there had been a shortage of male teachers, and had been there ever since. She spoke French with a strong Caledonian accent; but she taught it well. The set books that we studied were usually selected from the works of Molière, Racine, or Corneille. Methods of language-teaching being what they were in those days, it would have been too much to hope that we might learn to speak French, but Miss Roberts taught us to read and understand it tolerably well.

At Weymouth the usual Public School plan was followed of dividing the school into two 'Sides', Classical and Modern. Boys on the Classical side were supposed to be intended for one or other of the learned professions; the Moderns were supposed to be aspiring to careers in commerce, engineering, science or the Armed Forces. Latin and Greek were, naturally, not on their curriculum. The Classical students, however, had two periods of Science – one of Physics, the other of Chemistry – each week. I was entered on the Classical side. None of the Classical boys, as far as I know, had any interest in Science at all. In fact, we all affected to view Science as something not quite genteel: an attitude from which I have never quite succeeded in freeing myself. Science bored us, and we made no effort to conceal our boredom.

The senior science master, Gerald Hamilton, an unkempt, stocky, yellow-haired Ulsterman, knew this, and made little effort to get us to take his subjects seriously. We used mildly to enjoy playing about with chemicals and bunsen burners. Chemistry we regarded as something of a joke, and various near-accidents used to occur. Physics interested us not at all, and made us restless; so on physics day Hammie, as we used to call him among ourselves, was often content to get us sitting down quietly in the tiered lecture room, writing what he called a 'comic essay'. These comic essays were mildly scurrilous exercises in fiction in which members of the school's staff – Hamilton himself excepted – were gently satirized, under thinly disguised names, and placed in a variety of ludicrous situations. It would be difficult to say which most enjoyed these farcical narratives, Mr Hamilton or ourselves.

We were careful not too far to exceed the bounds of licence; but a day came when I took too large a risk in a story chiefly aimed at Lionel Gough. There was no malice in this; I liked Gough and got on well with him. He was an easy target because of his unusual appearance. He was quite a young man, and yet was completely bald, with a high-domed forehead. (After he had left Weymouth he wore a wig.) Horace Moule, Uncle Ernest's brother, appeared in the story, but was let down rather more lightly. I knew that this time I had gone a bit far in my satire; and I guessed that Hamilton would show the story to Gough, for they were on very friendly terms. But I reasoned that either Gough would not recognize himself, or, if he did, that he would not do anything about it, because he would not want anyone else to see it. But I was wrong. Gough not only read the story, he took it to the Headmaster. The result was that I received six of the best, as we used to say, and lost my much prized job as school librarian. However, the affair did not seem to have provoked any ill will. Gough may even have been amused as well as aggrieved. At any rate, my manuscript was neither destroyed nor returned to me. Later it got into the hands of the chaplain, Victor Tanner. Some years after I had left the school I learned that he still had it. I would very much like to be able to read it again, if only to see whether it was as funny as I thought it at the time. Since then I have produced a large quantity of miscellaneous journalism and have written several books; but I have never again essayed the medium of fiction.

Among the chief subjects of study on the Classical side at Weymouth were, of course, Latin and Greek, which were taught by Mr Conway and Dr Moule. Virgil was our principal author in Latin, Thucydides in Greek. H.F. Moule was known in scholarly circles as the co-author, with T.H. Darlow, of the great bibliography of English versions of the Bible, known as 'Darlow and Moule'. Mr Conway and Dr Moule were both fine scholars and good teachers, so that we made reasonable (if not *good*) progress under their tuition. Like his brother, Uncle Ernest, Horace Moule was a tall man, but he had a kind of Pickwickian amiability which was very different from his brother's manner. He was afflicted with a stammer which could be troublesome to him at times, and his classes were sometimes a little disorderly; but there was a point, as there was with Mr Major, beyond which it was not safe to try him.

I once attempted to tease 'the Doc', as we called him, by displaying on my desk a copy of *Blackfriars*, the Dominican monthly review, of which I had got to know through the advertise-ment columns of Chesterton's paper, *G.K.'s Weekly*, to which Gough had introduced us. This earned me the magisterial rebuke, delivered with a slight stutter: "Put that away, Sewell. We don't want any of that Anglo-Catholic stuff here." I was disappointed that he had failed to identify the magazine as Roman Catholic, which might have drawn a sharper reproof.

Since Weymouth College was a specifically Anglican foundation religion played a big part in the school's life. On weekdays there was a short service in the chapel every morning, and on Sundays there was always Sung Mattins with sermon at 11 a.m. The Holy Communion was celebrated on one Sunday only in each month. The chapel was arranged in the collegiate manner, with rows of pews facing each other across a central aisle, with a single pew for visitors placed at the west end. The communion table stood in the cord of the apse; on it there were no lights, only a plain brass cross. The services were uniformly 'low'. The chaplain, the Reverend E.V. Tanner, MA, MC, celebrated the eucharist in choir dress: surplice, scarf and academic hood, standing at the north end of the holy table. The use of vestments, even of linen chasubles, would have been unthinkable. From time to time Gough would urge Tanner to be bold and introduce coloured stoles; but any such attempt would have been vetoed by the Board of Governors.

Victor Tanner has been described as one of the great schoolmasters of the present century, which possibly he was. His sermons, as I recall them, did not have any great doctrinal content, but paid much attention to the virtues of clean, manly living, and the cultivation of fair play. His divinity classes I found extremely tedious: they seemed always to be about Tiglathpilesar, Assurbanipal, and other Babylonian and Assyrian Old Testament potentates. However, there were those who professed to find these classes interesting. Tanner was the housemaster at College House, which faced the school's main building. A boy in his house whom he thought looked dejected admitted under questioning, but without naming anyone, that he was being bullied. Tanner's reply was: "Well, perhaps it's good for character." When the boy replied that he had no wish to acquire the kind of character implied, Tanner offered no further comment.

An attractive feature of life at Weymouth College was the lectures, often lantern lectures, for we were still in the era of the 'magic lantern', and concerts that took place from time to time, usually in the evening. There was an elderly gentleman entertainer, Mr Chester, who came once a year,and was a great favourite both with the boys and with the staff. Mr Chester had a large repertoire of stories, jokes and songs, all of which he seemed to enjoy as much as his audience did. Among his songs I remember Sterndale

Bennett's *Dashing away with the Smoothing Iron* and one about *The Little Tin Soldier and his Tin Gee-gee*. This latter song was a special favourite with Mr and Mrs Conway.

These entertainments took place after supper, in the big first floor room or hall where we did our prep, under the stern supervision of one of the prefects. For lectures, the desks and benches were cleared away, and chairs put out, by the school's janitor, 'Gary' Cooper, who was not unlike the famous film star, and his assistant Harry Chick, who was subject to 'turns': perhaps an inheritance from the 1914 war. One day it was announced in class that a clergyman, the Reverend Runnells Moss, would shortly be coming to the school to give a Dickens recital. Lionel Gough had been teaching some of us to appreciate Dickens; we had been reading in class a very amusing episode from *Our Mutual Friend* concerning Silas Wegg, Mr Venus and their 'friendly move'. But most of the school, and especially the 'hearty' element, was thrown into a frenzy by this announcement, and great resentment was expressed at the prospect of what was expected to be a stupendously boring evening. The fact that there would be no 'homework' on that evening seemed to make no difference.

On the appointed evening tempers were running quite high. When the lecturer appeared on the platform he was seen to be a very portly, bland-looking clergyman in a light grey suit. (Some of us had strict ideas about clerical dress; for instance, we condemned out of hand the wearing of ordinary trousers, instead of apron and gaiters, by visiting colonial bishops.) Light grey we thought very unbecoming in a clergyman's suiting. Even the few 'Dickensians' in the audience now began to feel misgivings. After the Headmaster had introduced him Mr Runnells Moss announced that he was going to tell us the story of *Martin Chuzzlewit*. The very name Chuzzlewit seemed to be unfavourably received; there were murmurings and mutterings, and much shuffling of feet; so much so that Mr Conway had to walk up and down the central aisle in order to secure quiet. The lecturer seemed unperturbed; perhaps he was used to this kind of reception?

However, once the narrator had begun to tell the story it was not long before you could have heard the proverbial pin drop. He told the story, a gripping one certainly, with great skill and panache, and seemed to know the whole book by heart. Without the aid

of costumes, properties, or make-up, he brought all Dickens's
characters before us in the most amazing way. We were no longer
looking at a fat, semi-elderly clergyman; we saw and heard only Mr
Pecksniff, Jonas Chuzzlewit, old Martin Chuzzlewit, Mark Tapley,
Tom and Ruth Pinch, Mrs Gamp, Mrs Todgers, and all the other
characters, each speaking in his or her individual tones and
accents. The performance was a real *tour de force*. I have seen and
heard nothing like it since.

When it was over the applause was thunderous. Mr Moss was
obviously delighted. When the applause had died down he said:
"Thank you, boys. As an encore I shall now give you my impression of a frog that has fallen into a bowl of cream". Which he
did. This earned for him an even more resounding ovation. Without
doubt Runnells Moss was a very gifted man. One wonders what his
pulpit appearances were like? Possibly not unlike those of Canon
Floodgaye in Osbert Sitwell's novel *Before the Bombardment*.

At Weymouth College the frequent classes in PT were only
mildly disagreeable, though tedious. They were held in the gymnasium, under the auspices of Sergeant-Major Bignell, the retired
veteran of many campaigns, we were given to understand, who ran
the OTC under the command of Captain Walkinton, the history
master, of whose military record nothing was known. 'Biggy', a
genial and modest man, who owned a tobacco and sweets shop
down by the harbour, never alluded to his own military career. He
had a line in gentle sarcasm which, unlike Ernest Moule's more
polished shafts, upset no one. For example, he would now and
then affect amazement when contemplating the physique of some
scrawny boy, and would exclaim: "The muscles of his brawny arms
stood out like sparrows' kneecaps." This echo of Henry Wadsworth
Longfellow never failed to amuse.

I have been told by an eye-witness of an incident in the gymnasium of which I was the protagonist. It has long faded from my
memory, but the witness is reliable. One of the exercises that I
most disliked, because I was so bad at it, was vaulting over that
piece of gymnastic equipment known as a vaulting horse. The thing
was always too high for me, and I could never get over it without an
unseemly scramble. On this occasion Biggy for some reason had to
leave the gym for a few minutes. No sooner had he left than I
removed the horse's detachable cover and got into the empty space

below it, where there was just room for one to curl up while another boy replaced the cover. I felt confident that the veteran of many campaigns would not notice my absence. He soon returned, and everyone began vaulting over the horse again. It trembled as they hurled themselves onto it, it was very stuffy inside, and I soon began to feel distinctly queasy. There was nothing else for it: I was obliged to disclose myself and painfully emerge. (Could I have got the notion of concealment, I wonder, from the story of the Trojan horse, familiar to us from our classical studies?)

Towards the end of my time at Weymouth College, in 1927 I think, Mr and Mrs Conway retired. I did not take to the new head-master, A.G. Pite, a son of the distinguished architect Professor Beresford Pite, who not long before had given us a stupendously boring lantern lecture on the architecture of the Renaissance. I conceived a prejudice against the new headmaster well before his arrival. It was rumoured that he had had no previous teach-ing experience, although he was a graduate, and had previously been employed as secretary to the Student Christian Movement, a publishing enterprise reputed to be decidedly Protestant. (This estimate was probably unfair, as was my general attitude to Pite, who proved to be a kind man, deeply concerned for the welfare of all the boys under his authority.) But now it was time for me, although I was only sixteen, to leave the school. The small preparatory school at Birchington-on-Sea which my father had acquired was in financial difficulties, so that he could no longer afford to pay my fees at Weymouth.

As I look back sixty-three years later I feel grateful for my time at Weymouth College. The school imparted an excellent education, and one's time there was, on balance, more agreeable than dis-agreeable. My chief friend there, Alick Newell, one of three brothers in the school, has been dead a good many years now. At the school he had, like myself, 'Roman' leanings, and after he had married a daughter of the senior music master at Beaumont, the public school run by the Society of Jesus, he became a Catholic. Another Weymouthian friend of mine, George Down, a day boy, later practised dentistry in Harley Street, and is now, in his retire-ment, one of the country's leading judges at dog shows. Ted Barnes, another day boy, pursued a military and then a scholastic career, and now lives close to his ancestral acres at Broadway, between

Weymouth and Dorchester, and possesses an expert knowledge of the history and interpretation of Gregorian chant. He has resisted the blandishments of Rome, and has remained faithful to the Anglo-Catholicism he professed even while he was being educated under the aegis of the Evangelical Church Schools trust.

Life is full of lost opportunities, and an opportunity that I missed at Weymouth was that of meeting Thomas Hardy, who was living only eight miles away at Max Gate, the gloomy house that he designed for himself just outside Dorchester. Hardy and the second Mrs Hardy, Florence Dugdale, were hospitable people, and Horace Moule could certainly have given me a letter of introduction, since he was a nephew of Hardy's friend and mentor, the Horace Moule who committed suicide in his rooms at Queen's College, Cambridge, in September 1874. I was aware of Hardy, of course, and his works were in the school library, but I do not think I had read any of them at that time.

CHAPTER THREE

'G.k.'s Weekly' and Life in London

ONE of the best things at Weymouth College was the library. Until Gough arrived Major had been in charge of the library, whose contents did not amount to much: plenty of Henty, Kingston, Ballantyne, and that kind of thing, but not much else. When Gough asked Major if he would like him to take over the library, Major was delighted. Gough managed to transform it quite quickly into a very good collection of books. The school's strongly Protestant ethos seemed less obtrusive in the library. On its shelves were novels, essays, and biographies by Belloc and Chesterton, Newman's *Apologia* – in the Everyman's Library edition – Father D'Arcy's *Roman Catholicism* – in Benn's Sixpenny Library. While still at school I went through a brief Anglo-Catholic phase, the result, to some extent, of my reading, and an encounter in a train, when returning from the school holidays, with a Father of the Society of the Sacred Mission, from Kelham. During the holidays I took to worshipping at Saint Augustine's, Kilburn, a magnificent Gothic Revival church by J.L. Pearson, with the tallest spire in London and a fine peal of bells. The principal service on Sunday mornings was the solemn eucharist or high mass, celebrated with stately ceremonial and the use of incense.

I now spent my school holidays, or the greater part of them, at Birchington House, the small school my father had acquired in the Isle of Thanet. Here I used on Sundays to attend the little Roman Catholic church of Our Lady and Saint Benedict. My father did not approve of this, quite naturally; but he did not forbid it. Anglo-Catholicism was soon left firmly behind. This little mission church with a corrugated iron roof was obviously a temporary structure. It has long since been replaced by a larger and more pretentious

edifice, of no great architectural merit. The furnishings and orna-
ments in this earlier conventicle were of no great beauty, but they
were unpretentious and devotional. Considering the parish's small
financial resources – it really relied on the offerings of the summer
seaside visitors to keep it going – the Sung Mass on Sunday
mornings was not at all badly managed. There was a small 'mixed'
choir which rendered very creditably the antiphons 'Asperges me'
and 'Vidi aquam' during their respective seasons, and at the
Offertory the choir could rise to the simpler kind of polyphonic
motet. At the evening service of Benediction the congregation sang
'O Salutaris' and 'Tantum ergo' with considerable verve, the Litany
of Loreto being rendered to cheerful settings by modern composers
such as Tozer and Terry.

At this time the Roman Catholic parishes in the Isle of Thanet
were served, as one or two of them still are, by Benedictine monks
of the Cassinese Congregation of the Primitive Observance from
Ramsgate Abbey. During the late nineteen twenties the parish
priest at Birchington was Dom Augustine Keniry, a cheerful monk
with a cockney accent. At the Sunday evening service in the summer he would often say: "The sun is shining; I know you all want to
get down to the beach to enjoy it. We won't have any sermon; we'll
just have a little meditation." When you heard the words 'a little
meditation' you knew that you could settle back in your seat for the
next twenty to thirty minutes. The next thing to listen for was: "But
the candles are burning down, the candles are burning down!" This
was the sign that Father Keniry's dis- course, always worth hearing,
was coming to an end. The rector of Birchington, Canon Serres,
used to describe Father Keniry, if his name came up in conversation, as 'active', which no doubt was a polite way of saying that he
found him a nuisance; for Father Keniry was a sociable man, and
made a point of knowing, as far as possible, everyone in his parish,
whether they were his parishioners or not.

When my father told me that I would soon have to leave school
because he could no longer afford the fees, I had no idea what I
would do when that time came. It must have been a disappointment
to him that my education had to be cut short; but in any case there
seemed to be no possibility of my going to a university, not only
because of the expense, but because of my inability to cope with
even the simplest mathematics. In the School Certificate examin-

ation in 1927 I had been awarded nil out of three hundred for maths.: nil for arithmetic, nil for algebra, nil for geometry. For admission to Oxford or Cambridge a certain level of competence in mathematics was required. In those days there were no careers masters or mistresses in the public schools, and no one told me that in the London University matriculation exam logic could be substituted for maths, as I discovered about twenty years later, with satisfactory results. The Church was ruled out for me as a possible profession because my religious opinions were so unsettled. The Bar, to which I was attracted, was ruled out because of the high fees that had to be paid if one were to qualify. The Armed Forces made no appeal. But I had seen in *G.K.'s Weekly* an advertisement which appeared each week from a group of craftsmen on Ditchling Common, in Sussex. There were four or five of these workshops, the last on the list being 'H.D.C. Pepler, printer, Saint Dominic's Press'. And it was stated that there were vacancies for apprentices. I began to wonder if printing might not be an interesting occupation; so I addressed a letter of inquiry to Mr Pepler, and received in reply an invitation to visit him during the coming summer holidays.

So one day in August 1928 I took a train from Victoria Station, in London, to Burgess Hill, on the Brighton line. From Burgess Hill I set out to walk the two miles to Ditchling Common by way of Folders Lane. A hundred yards or so before the crossroads in the middle of Ditchling Common a sign on the righthand side of the lane indicated a path leading to the workshops of the Guild of Saint Joseph and Saint Dominic, the fellowship of Catholic craftsmen founded in 1920 by Hilary Pepler and Eric Gill. Gill had left in 1924. The workshops, most of them wooden ex-Army huts, were grouped around a grass plot or quadrangle on whose further side was a two-storey brick building which a small sign identified as Saint Dominic's Press. Having knocked on the door and been bidden to enter I was greeted by Mr Pepler himself, a tall, handsome man, of rather grave mien, but with a twinkle in his eye which seemed indicative of good humour. He was fifty years old, but scarcely looked it. His speech was measured and thoughtful; this hinted, perhaps, at his Quaker upbringing, of which I knew nothing. But I did know that he was a Roman Catholic, and I believe he was the first lay Catholic I had met.

On entering the Saint Dominic's Press workshop I found myself in a new world. I had some vague idea of what an ordinary small-town printer's premises looked like, but here was something quite different. Saint Dominic's Press was one of a number of 'private presses' then flourishing; but its aims were more modest than those of the larger private presses, such as Robert Gibbings's Golden Cockerel Press, at Waltham Saint Lawrence, or the Gregynog Press at Newtown, Montgomeryshire. Douglas Pepler's original aim – he adopted the name Hilary only after his baptism – was simply to print whatever his customers might require of him and to publish books on traditional crafts that might be in danger of disappearing. He believed, perhaps not quite correctly, that any fool can learn to print, and he preferred to use handpresses rather than machines because the handpress gives the printer greater control over his product.

The front door of Saint Dominic's Press opened directly into the composing room, from which an open arch led into the press-room. Here I saw, for the first time, iron handpresses, the immediate successors to the old wooden presses used by Gutenberg and Caxton. There was a Stanhope press of 1790, the Stanhope being the earliest of the iron handpresses. This one was said to have belonged to William Morris at his Kelmscott Press. There was also a folio Albion; and a Columbian, a press of American origin. On the south wall of the press-room were displayed some of the posters that had been printed on these presses; posters of a bold simplicity and originality of design that set them quite apart from the ordinary run of 'commercial' posters. Some of them were embellished with wood-engravings by Eric Gill, David Jones, Desmond Chute, and other artists.

In 1928 the typeface still in almost exclusive use at Saint Dominic's Press was Caslon Old Face, an eighteenth century type that has few rivals for beauty and clarity. Later, other typefaces were used, but sparingly. The type was set by hand, though for bigger jobs the facilities of Monotype were sometimes made use of; mostly when it was a matter of printing really big books, such as Margaret Douglas's *Selected Writings* and *The Natural Moral Law*, a doctoral thesis by Father Walter Farrell, OP.

Within a few minutes of my arrival Mr Pepler had handed me a composing stick and begun to teach me to set type by hand. He was a good instructor, and I seemed to show some aptitude. A day or two later, at the end of my visit, he said that he would be willing to take me as an apprentice if I applied. But in the event I did not apply, which perhaps in a way was a mistake. For after I got back to school I was smitten with a passion for journalism, and wrote to ask if there was any possibility of my getting a job on *G.K.'s Weekly*. I was told that as it happened there would shortly be a vacancy, and it was this offer that I accepted. But, though I did not know it, I had not seen the last of Mr Pepler and Saint Dominic's Press.

The post with *G.K.'s Weekly* fell vacant in October, so I left school in the middle of the autumn term, at the age of sixteen, and entered the nation of London. It had been arranged that I should live with my uncle Glynn Grylls and his family in Woolwich Dockyard, where he was the officer commanding the Royal Army Ordnance Corps. From Monday to Friday of each week I went up to London by train each morning to the offices shared by *G.K.'s Weekly* and its supporting organization the Distributist League, two rooms at the top of a ricketty old eighteenth century building in Little Essex Street, off the Strand and close to Fleet Street. Here I worked chiefly under the direction of Mr G.C. Heseltine, a director of the company which published the *Weekly*, and the first and last paid secretary of the Distributist League. *G.K.'s Weekly* was the official organ of the League, which had been formed in 1926 to propagate the economic doctrine known as Distributism, an alternative to Capitalism and Socialism, which had been formulated as long ago as 1912 by Hilaire Belloc. George Heseltine was a combative Yorkshireman; a thoroughly likeable man, he was by profession an author and journalist, but he had also had experience of farming. In the war of 1914-1918 he had been a pilot in the Royal Flying Corps. He was a ready and forceful public speaker, and was well qualified to run an organization such as the Distributist League. Unfortunately, the League had been hastily contrived, and had built-in faults for which Heseltine was not responsible. These were serious enough to prevent its becoming a really effective national movement. It was inadequately funded, the annual membership subscription was far too low, and it lacked vigorous leadership at the top. Mr Chesterton, the President, was unable, for reasons of health and temperament, to assume the rôle of an active leader, and Mr Belloc was unwilling to take up again the political life that he had abandoned in 1912. Nevertheless, the Distributist movement, of which the League was the nucleus, achieved more than biographers of Chesterton and Belloc have given it credit for.

In the office of *G.K.'s Weekly* I was a kind of general factotum; in the Distributist League's office I was something rather more; in fact, I was in sole charge whenever Mr Heseltine was away, as he often was, addressing meetings up and down the country. At such times I had to deal with correspondence, as far as I was able, answer telephone calls, acknowledge subscriptions and donations, and do what I could to meet the needs of people, inquirers and others, who called. On Wednesday afternoons I had to go to Euston Station to collect the bundles of copies of the new number of the *Weekly*, which arrived by train from the printers at Nuneaton. It was my job to bring them back to the office by taxi, delivering some of the larger bundles to firms of wholesale newsagents on the way. Since all the bundles of copies could be got into one taxi it will be surmised that the paper's circulation was not large. In fact, it never got beyond eight thousand copies, and was often less than that. Back at the office my next duty was to put the postal subscribers' copies into their already addressed wrappers, and get them into the post as quickly as possible. From routine duties of this kind I was gradually advanced to writing an occasional paragraph on current affairs for the 'Notes of the Week' feature, and from time to time I would be asked to contribute a book review.

Our editor, Mr Chesterton, we saw once a month only, apart from his occasional appearance at Distributist meetings in London. Although a Londoner by birth and temperament he lived, for reasons of health, in the ancient town of Beaconsfield, some twenty miles to the north-west of the capital. With his great size and girth, the ascent of our steep and shaky old staircase was trying for him, and we could hear him wheezing and groaning on his way up, until he came through the office door and sank into the editorial swivel-chair, which was just, but only just, big enough and strong enough to support him. His 'absentee' editorship worked very well, for there was an assistant editor in charge on the spot who put the paper together each week and saw it through the press. Mr Chesterton's 'copy' – he contributed a full-page article and two shorter ones every week, and often a book review or a note on current affairs as well – always arrived in good time by post, or, if he had been delayed in writing it, by train, from which I collected it at Marylebone station. The contents of each number he always discussed over the telephone with the assistant editor.

The first assistant-editor was W.R. Titterton, a veteran Fleet Street journalist who had been a regular contributor to Belloc's paper *The Eye- Witness* and to Cecil Chesterton's *The New Witness*. Titterton was by temperament a Romantic, and Gilbert Chesterton was his great hero. Under Titterton's care *G.K.'s Weekly* had a liveliness which it never quite regained after he left, and was succeeded by a younger man, Edward Macdonald, who was a man of great competence and integrity, but had not Titterton's gift for satirizing the great and powerful, and for breaking out into humorous rhyming couplets printed as if they were prose.

Titterton had left not long before my arrival on the scene. By then Edward Macdonald had the assistance of a kind of informal editorial board, made up of young Distributists, among whom was Edward's brother Gregory, a freelance journalist and Oxford gradu- ate who had made himself an authority on Poland and Polish affairs, to which Mr Chesterton, a great friend to the Polish nation, wished his paper to give special attention.

When he appeared in the office our editor was always in genial mood, for he enjoyed being in London, and his conversation was always of a rare brilliance, and highly entertaining. I think Chesterton's conversation must have been even better than Oscar Wilde's; but it has been less well recorded. Wilde was not really a conversationalist; more of a solo performer. Chesterton's jests and quips were spontaneous; Wilde's were often carefully prepared beforehand, and held in reserve until opportunity for their use arose. While with us, Mr Chesterton would usually drink one small glass of sherry and smoke a cheroot, while doodling on a blank sheet of paper. These doodlings were mostly sketches or cartoons of real or imaginary beings, very much in the vein of the drawings that he did as illustrations to Hilaire Belloc's novels. The Old Man, as we called him when he was not present, always left these doodlings behind when he departed, and Gregory Macdonald always gathered them up. They must today be a valuable collection.

In 1930 a meeting of the Central (London) Branch of the Distributist League elected me honorary secretary of their Com-

mittee. My election to this post at the age of seventeen would seem
to show that I had impressed the members as being someone of
potential ability. One of the secretary's duties was to organize the
Central Branch's programme of lectures and other events for the
coming session, from September to May, of public meetings. The
London Distributists met on Friday evenings at The Devereux, a
pub just off Essex Street and close to The Temple, the meetings
being advertized in *G.K.'s Weekly*. The speakers were not always
Distributists, and quite often represented other social and political
creeds. The talk, or lecture, usually of thirty to fifty minutes, would
be followed by a general discussion, after which the chairman
would sum up and propose a vote of thanks. When the meeting
was over, most of those present would adjourn to the bar down-
stairs, where the discussion might well continue informally until
closing time. The average attendance at these meetings would
probably be about thirty; sometimes there would be more, and a well
known speaker, such as Father Vincent McNabb, the Dominican,
might attract upwards of a hundred, when it would be a matter of
'standing room only'. At least once in every session there would
be a debate between some prominent Distributist, perhaps Mr
Chesterton, Mr Belloc, or Fr McNabb, and some other well known
public figure. These debates were usually held in the Essex Hall, at
the Unitarians' headquarters in Essex Street, which could hold
between four and five hundred people.

Our guest-speakers on Friday evenings included Fabians and
other kinds of Socialist, Individualists, advocates of Social Credit,
supporters of the Henry George 'Single Tax' movement, British
Fascists – just then beginning to come into prominence – the
Rural Reconstruction Association, the Catholic Land Movement,
and others. Among the better known speakers whom I invited were
the Marquess of Tavistock (the future Duke of Bedford), leader of
the Social Credit movement and founder of the minuscule British
People's Party; Father Vincent McNabb; and Father St John Groser,
a leading member of Conrad Noel's christian-communist Catholic
Crusade. There was also Eric Gill, who spoke on the subject of
printing and book production, reading passages from the proofs of
his forthcoming book, *An Essay on Typography*. This was my first
meeting with Gill, whom later I was to come to know well.

Among the younger Distributists who frequented The Devereux

at that time were Dunstan Pruden, silversmith, who later joined the Guild of Saint Joseph and Saint Dominic at Ditchling, Anthony Foster, the future sculptor and assistant to Eric Gill, his younger brother Francis, the future Dominican, who was later Reader in Italian Studies at Oxford University, and John Hawkswell, the future founder of two 'back-to-the-land' communities.

On one particular Friday evening Hawkswell was the speaker at The Devereux. He gave his hearers an impassioned denunciation of the evils of modern urban and industrial life, and concluded with a rousing exhortation to his audience to shake off the dust of London from their feet and take to a life of peasant small-holding ownership in the English countryside. This was, in reality, something for which most of those present were totally unfitted. However, Hawkswell's words fell on good ground. I had noticed in the audience a little old lady who seemed to be a stranger. After the meeting she approached the speaker, and said: "Mr Hawkswell, you are right. We must act. Tomorrow I shall send you a cheque for two thousand pounds." Which she did. With this money Hawkswell bought several thousand acres of land – much of it marsh, but the rest of it good wheat-growing soil – at Langenhoe, in Essex. There he settled, to farm the land, and was joined by his benefactress, Mrs Judges, a clergyman's widow, and her two daughters, one of whom he married.

The Distributists were mostly, as was natural with followers of Belloc and Chesterton, Roman Catholics, but by no means all of them were of the Roman obedience. The League's founder, Captain H.S.D. Went, late of the Royal Marines, was a High Tory Anglo-Catholic; John Cargill, civil engineer, a Scot, was Presbyterian; and E.H. Haywood, a high-ranking official of the Workers' Travel Association, was a declared Freethinker. However, when I left school I already had a strong disposition towards Catholicism, and in the world of *G.K.'s Weekly* and Distributism that disposition could hardly but be strengthened.

After a year or so in London, by which time I knew my way about the city, I began to feel a need for greater independence. My aunt Kitty, in Woolwich, of whom I was very fond, had a friend, an elderly lady, who lived in a boarding house in Cecile Park, N8, in the borough of Hornsey, to which I was able to move. Here I had a pleasant small room, with breakfast and evening meal every day, and full board at weekends: all for thirty shillings a week. (My total salary was £3 a week.) The nearest Catholic church to Cecile Park, and it was quite near at hand, was Saint Peter-in-Chains, Stroud Green. This church was served by a community of Austin Canons, of the Lateran Congregation, which had its headquarters in Rome. In the late nineteen twenties there were six or seven canons at Saint Peter's, a not unpleasing neo-Gothic structure from the designs of Canon Scoles, a secular priest who was a qualified architect. The prior of the community at Saint Peter's was Dom Aloysius Smith, titular Abbot of Leicester; that is, of the ruined abbey where Cardinal Wolsey had died. Abbot Smith was a quiet, gentle man, of scholarly bent. He was averse to display, and pontificated with mitre and crozier on rare occasions only. He was a man of prayer, a good preacher, and possessed administrative ability.

His second-in-command, Dom Gilbert Higgins, was a man of some distinction too. For services to his Order he had been created titular Prior of Bridlington, and he was an honorary canon of Rouen. He was a renowned preacher in both English and French. Among the other canons regular at Stroud Green in 1929 were Dom Philip Gresham-Brown, a former Discalced Carmelite friar who was a gifted artist and pianist, and Dom Norbert Jones, a lovable eccentric, of Franciscan tendencies, whom the Abbot had sometimes to restrain from giving away most of his clothes to the poor.

At Saint Peter-in-Chains on Sundays things were done well. The solemn sung Vespers in the evening taught me to love the psalms in the Vulgate Latin, and the ancient plainsong tones to which they were sung.

In the parish there were some other young men who were Distributists and frequented The Devereux: Aemon Dunne, an Irish nationalist who taught in the Working Men's College in Crowndale Road, Kentish Town; Sean Egan, another keen member of the Gaelic League; Pat Jacob, who worked in an office in the City; and Wilfrid Roser, a convert from Nonconformity, who joined the Canons Regular, and died only a few years after his ordination. Sometimes on a fine Sunday evening we would desert Saint Peter's for some other church: it might be Saint Joseph's, the great copper-domed church of the Passionist Fathers on Highgate Hill, or Saint Dominic's Priory, the church of the Blackfriars in Southampton

Road, NW5. Saint Dominic's is one of the biggest churches in London, a huge neo-Gothic fane: a considerable white elephant today, one would suppose. Here one witnessed the ceremonial of the Dominican rite, a good deal more elaborate and *mouvementé* than the sober ritual of the Roman rite.

The senior choir-stall in the sanctuary at Saint Dominic's was occupied, unless he were away, by the prior provincial, Father Bede Jarrett, then at the height of his fame as a preacher, which extended to the other side of the Atlantic. Facing him, on the other side of the choir, would be the prior, Father Antoninus Maguire, who somehow always managed to convey an impression of 'worldliness'; partly because he took a keen interest in the congregation, always a very large one, and often glanced down the church to see who was there. He was always almost excessively well groomed, with conspicuously well cared for hair, not a strand out of place. When in secular clerical dress he was always immaculately got up, with the sharpest of creases in his trousers, and his shoes polished to a nicety. But if he were wanted for any reason, and could not be found in his cell, he was usually to be discovered in the church, at his prayers. It seems that he was like that even as a novice, and then as a student-friar. Which shows how careful we should be not to judge simply by appearances.

At Compline on Sunday evenings Father Jarrett and Father McNabb were frequent preachers, and people came from considerable distances to hear them. Father Bede well deserved his fame as a preacher, and many of his sermons were published. He had a beautiful, silver-toned voice. In the pulpit he stood erect, perfectly still, with his arms folded under his scapular. Father Vincent's manner was very different. This gaunt, bald, bony friar – the local *gamins* nicknamed him 'Gandhi' – spoke in a Northern Irish accent; in the pulpit he was restless, and made use of many gestures; he was not above playing to the gallery. You never knew what to expect from him. He might give a simple yet profound meditation on a passage from the Gospel, an impassioned denunciation of the evils of industrialism and modern urban life, or a brilliantly satirical display of verbal fireworks, with shafts of humour or irony that would set the whole congregation laughing. By this time Father McNabb was a national figure, familiar too in the streets of the capital, where he walked everywhere in the habit of his Order. He knew a great many people, high and low, and was actually sent for by the Archbishop of Canterbury, Randall Davidson, when he lay dying at Lambeth Palace. He held the coveted degree of Master of Sacred Theology, and yet had been gravely suspect by the Holy Office in Rome earlier in the century on account of his 'advanced' views on biblical questions. Father Vincent McNabb died in 1943, aged seventy- two, and still there is no biography of this extraordinary man.

In Holy Week each year one went to Westminster Cathedral, not then the tawdry place it has since become, or else to Pugin's Saint George's Cathedral, in Southwark, soon to be destroyed in the blitz. At Westminster Cardinal Bourne was a figure of great dignity as he presided at the solemn rites of the Great Week; but he had a poor singing voice. On Maundy Thursday, Good Friday, and Holy Saturday his two auxiliaries, Dr Joseph Butt, Bishop of Cambysopolis *in partibus infidelium*, and Dr Manoel Bidwell, Bishop of Miletopolis *i.p.i.* presided. Dr Butt was a grave and venerable prelate who looked as if he had stepped straight out of the eighteenth century; Dr Bidwell was of a less impressive appearance. It was currently said of this triumvirate that in the management of the diocese of Westminster the Cardinal supplied the element of holiness, Dr Butt that of courtly diplomacy, and Dr Bidwell that of low intrigue. But such sayings are not to be taken too seriously.

At Saint George's Cathedral there was a fine Holy Week tradition, but things were done there a little less elaborately than at Westminster. There was no choir school at Saint George's; but it could always rise to an occasion. The bishop, Dr Peter Emmanuel Amigo, had a fine presence; but he had a homely touch too. In the procession of the palms on Palm Sunday he would stop to speak to small children in the congregation, and before the solemn singing of the Passion he would always tell the old people not to stand all through it, but to sit down when they felt tired.

Nothing could be further from the truth than the now sedulously fostered idea that in the days of the Latin liturgy the people understood nothing of what was going on in church. I believe that even the less educated members of any congregation understood very well what was being done at Mass: the *anamnesis*, or calling to mind, and the offering of the One Sacrifice. The Latin mass-texts in

the layfolk's missals were printed in columns parallel with a translation; and the principal instructional parts of the Mass, the Lesson
and the Gospel, were always read from the pulpit in English. I
do not believe that present-day congregations, with their parrot-
fashion responses to the drab, modern-version 'responsorial psalm',
show any greater 'understanding' of the divine mysteries than did
the congregations of 'pre-conciliar' days. Rather less so, if anything.

CHAPTER FOUR

In Saint Dominic's Country

MY father had told me that he was not prepared to allow me to become a Catholic until I was twenty-one. This restriction was not unreasonable, but I found it irksome. However, in 1930, when I was eighteen, he withdrew it; which was magnanimous. So I was received into the Catholic and Roman church by Dom Gilbert Higgins, at the church of Saint Peter-in-Chains, after a six months' course of instruction, from which I learned little that I did not know already. On that occasion my sponsor or godfather was George Heseltine; Anthony and Francis Foster were the witnesses.

I never find the question, What made you become a Catholic? easy to answer. There were, of course, certain disposing factors; for instance, a reaction against the rather arid public school religion at Weymouth College, such a contrast to what went on in Saint Augustine's RC church a few hundred yards further up the Dorchester road. Also, I had come to question the claim of the Church of England to be 'the Catholic Church of this land'. The archbishops of Canterbury and York no longer wore the pallium, the symbol of communion with the Holy See, although it still appeared on their coats of arms. That seemed to me to indicate that there was something wrong somewhere. Anglican doctrinal confusion, and the toleration of Modernists such as Dr Barnes, the Bishop of Birmingham, and Dr Inge, the Dean of St Paul's, contrasted unfavourably with the seemingly monolithic unity and orthodoxy of the Roman church. Today, however, in the nineteen nineties, the Catholic church is equally confused, with division and hostility between 'conciliarists' and traditionalists. (By conciliarists are here meant the adherents of the Second Vatican

46

Council – *le néfaste concile*, as the abbé Georges de Nantes calls it – not those, among whom I number myself, who believe with the decree *Sacrosancta* of the Council of Constance (1414-1418) that a General Council of the Church 'is superior to everyone, of whatever rank and dignity, including the Pope'.

Roman Catholic historians usually betray a certain embarrassment when discussing the Council of Constance. They are not prepared to deny its ecumenical status, but make every shift to exclude the decree *Sacrosancta* from its authoritative pronouncements.

If in 1930 I had been able to foresee the state of the Roman church after the second Vatican Council, would I have become a Catholic? I think perhaps not. However, I believe, as did the early Church, that every Christian should be in communion with his or her patriarch. (The patriarchs are the bishops of sees founded by, or at least closely associated with, an apostle.) The bishop of Rome is the patriarch of the West, as successor of Saint Peter.

In the summer of 1930 I had been with *G.K.'s Weekly* and the Distributist League for about eighteen months, and I was by no means as content there as I had been to begin with. Perhaps I in some way sensed that the Distributist movement had no great future before it, and that Fleet Street was not my real element. But there had been changes. George Heseltine had resigned, for personal reasons, from the secretaryship of the League; but also because the League could no longer afford to pay his salary. It was badly underfunded; and no wonder, since the annual subscription had been fixed at one shilling. Heseltine was succeeded by Francis W. Osborne, a middle-aged civil servant in Whitehall, who was honorary secretary, and could attend in the office on a part-time basis only. In fact, he was not much in evidence, and this made things rather lonely for me. Also, I did not get on very well with Van Norman Lucas, *G.K.'s Weekly*'s business manager. Lucas was not a Catholic, whereas the Macdonald brothers were; but this can hardly be the explanation of the lack of rapport between us.

The next thing was that Osborne quite unexpectedly resigned. This was a blow to me, as we had worked well together; but his chiefs in Whitehall had told him that he must either give up his position with the Distributist League or else leave the Civil Service. Presumably some misguided person in Whitehall must have thought that the Distributist movement was a threat to national security, or something like that.

Osborne was succeeded by F. Keston Clarke, a schools attendance officer whose clever short stories were published in the London *Evening News* and the *Argosy* magazine, as well as in *G.K.'s Weekly*. Keston Clarke was duly succeeded by other part-time honorary secretaries.

When Heseltine went, the real driving force behind the League went with him, and my days in the office became very desultory. In this unsettling and unsettled state of things it was natural that my thoughts should turn to fresh woods and pastures new. But where were these to be found?

Perhaps it was inevitable that my thoughts should turn towards the monastic life and the priesthood. After all, the Sewells were a highly clerical family, and so, indeed, were the Gryllses. No doubt there was a degree of romanticism in this attraction to the clergy; but as Saint Augustine says, God can write straight on crooked lines. I was especially drawn to the Dominicans. I consulted Dom Gilbert Higgins, and he saw no reason why I should not apply to them, which I did. There followed an interview with Father Bede Jarrett, and some days later I received a letter from him saying that he was prepared to allow me to enter the novitiate at Woodchester in a year's time, if I were still of the same mind.

The year of probation for young men wishing to join the English Dominican province always began on Holy Cross Day, 14th September; so on that day in 1931 I left London for Stroud, the nearest station to Woodchester, in Gloucestershire. At Paddington a tall young man of about my own age, or a little more, and a girl who looked as if she might be his sister, got into the same compartment of the train as myself. The young man noticed that I was reading a copy of *The Game*, a handprinted magazine edited betweeen 1916 and 1924 by Hilary Pepler and Eric Gill, and asked me if I had been to Ditchling or knew any of the people there. After that, conversation was easy. My two companions were on the same mission as I was, and were the son and daughter of Edward Bullough, professor of Italian at Cambridge, and his wife Enrichetta, a daughter of the actress Eleanora Duse. Professor and Mrs Bullough were Dominican tertiaries, and outstanding benefactors of the Order's English province. Their two children, Hugh and Leonora, were on

their way respectively to be novitiates at Woodchester Priory and
Saint Rose's Convent, Stroud.

Also on the train were some other intending novices; so in the
middle of the afternoon a bunch of young men made their way up
the steep hillside path to the Priory of the Annunciation, where
they were met and greeted by the novice-master, Father Eustace
O'Gorman, a curly-haired friar from Manchester who looked less
than his fifty-odd years. In all there were twelve of us postulants, or
prospective novices: this was the average yearly number of entrants
at the time. Among them was Anthony Foster, my ex-Downside
friend from The Devereux. Most of us were, I suppose, aged from
sixteen to about twenty-one. The oldest of the group, an Irishman
from Newcastle upon Tyne, was probably nearer thirty. He was a
nice enough fellow, but there was something about him that made
him a little difficult to get on with. He was the first of us to leave,
after a relatively short stay. By far the cleverest man among us was
Hugh Bullough, soon to be known as Brother Sebastian. He was a
Cambridge graduate, and already gave promise of the scholarly
distinction that he would later achieve. He was an entertaining conversationalist, with a vivacity of speech that he probably
inherited from his Italian mother. The oddity among us was a
certain Norbert Drewitt, best described, perhaps, as a 'brainy' man.
The rest of us arrived at Woodchester wearing the sort of decent
casual clothes that were suited to the occasion; Drewitt turned up
wearing a black suit, with dark shirt and black tie, and one of those
round clerical hats such as Chesterton's Father Brown is usually
depicted as wearing. Also, he was carrying an umbrella. To the
surprise of some he completed the course at Woodchester, and went
on to the house of studies in Staffordshire. Later, at Blackfriars,
Oxford, he became an adherent of the ideas of the psychologist
C.G. Jung. He duly reached ordination; but not many years later he
left the Order, and exercised the cure of souls in an Anglican
country parish. Before his death, however, he returned to the
Mother Church.

In 1930 the Priory of the Annunciation at Woodchester
was nearly a hundred years old; it was the first monastery the
Dominicans had been able to establish in England since Reformation times. It was a most attractive neo-Gothic building, designed
by Charles Hansom, the best (in partnership with his brother

Joseph) of the Gothic Revival men after Pugin. The monastery was
built on the traditional plan around three sides of a central garth,
the church filling the fourth side. The church had a small steeple,
housing three bells. When viewed from the road below, or from the
high ground on the other side of the Stroud Valley, the whole group
of buildings made a most pleasing picture.

In 1931 the interior of the priory was rather dingy, as if it had
not been painted for a good many years. In August 1932, after I
had left, the Master-General of the Order, the Most Reverend
Martin Stanislaus Gillet, a Frenchman, drew the prior and community's attention, in a document which he had prepared after
making a canonical visitation of the priory, to the bad state of the
building, and directed that appropriate steps be taken to deal with
it. It does not appear that much was done until about 1935, and
then perhaps not as much was done as should have been done. In
the nineteen fifties, however, the fabric seems to have been in fairly
good condition; and in 1964/5 two architects reported that it was
well worth doing up further. But dry rot set in, and this caused it
to be demolished in 1968, since the estimated cost of putting
things to rights, £100,000, was more than the Order could meet.
Fortunately the church remains; but the Dominicans have now
left the parish, which was never financially viable. As far back
as 1853, before the priory was even built, Matthew Bridges, the
author of the hymn 'Crown Him with many crowns', had declared
that this would be so.

On the evening of our arrival the community's annual eight day
retreat began, conducted by Father Bede Jarrett. During the retreat
the postulants were interviewed, one by one, by the Prior, Father
Robert Bracey, and his council, who questioned each one about
his reasons for wishing to become a Dominican. We had already
submitted testimonials from our respective parish priests; now we
had to give proof of sufficient education, for which purpose we were
each required to translate at sight a substantial passage from the
Latin of the Dominican breviary. This test we all passed.

During the retreat a state of near-silence prevailed in the house.
When it was over we were invested, each one kneeling before the
Prior in the chapter room, and in the presence of the community,
with the habit of the Order: white tunic, scapular, and capuce, with
the black *cappa* (or mantle) and black capuce that were worn in

choir during the winter, and by the fathers when preaching or giving retreats, or when otherwise wearing the habit in public.

We soon settled down to novitiate life. When we arrived, the previous year's novices, those that had survived, were still there; it was their helpful explanations that made it comparatively easy for us to adjust to claustral life. It was the dean, or senior, of these previous novices who initiated us into the complexities of the breviary, about which, with the exception of Brother Sebastian, we knew nothing. In the sixteenth century Cranmer had compiled an abridged and simplified breviary in the *Book of Common Prayer*. Trying to master the intricacies of the *Brevarium secundum ritum sacri Ordinis Praedicatorum*, I could see exactly what Cranmer meant when he said in his article 'Concerning the Service of the Church' that 'The number and hardness of the rules called the *Pie*, and the manifold changing of the service, was the cause, that to turn the book only was so hard and intricate a matter, that many times there was more business to find out what should be read, than to read it when it was found out.' However, since Cranmer's time the breviary had been much simplified. Once its basic plan was understood it did not take long to master it.

During their twelve probationary months the novices did no formal studies; the novitiate was supposed to be basically a year of spiritual formation. However, they were instructed by the Father Master in the life of prayer, and there were regular classes on the history and traditions of the Order, and on how to sing plain-chant. Also studied were the liturgical rite of the Order and its ceremonial. Classes were mostly held in the morning. In the after-noon, except on Sundays, and on Thursdays, when we went for a long walk in the countryside, we mostly worked in the large garden on the hillside behind the priory. Gardening I have always found tedious; but here the tedium could be relieved by conversation, which was not allowed, necessity apart, in the monastery except for a brief period after lunch, and again after supper. Silence was the rule in the refectory, even on Christmas Day, when the customary reading aloud from some approved book was dispensed with. The books read were usually works of church history or hagiography, though an occasional excursion into secular biography was not unknown. The silence could be dispensed from only by the Master of the Order, if he were present, the Minister-General of the Order

of Friars Minor (Franciscans), or the reigning monarch. The one
exception to this was that the prior could dispense in honour of a
visiting bishop.

Silence was strictly observed in the cloisters, the sacristy, and
the cells of the brethren, and it was an offence to enter another
friar's cell without permission. When we were gardening I always
enjoyed talking with Sebastian Bullough, because he knew all sorts
of interesting people, and had a lot of unusual information.

In those days canon law required that the novitiate should be
separate from other parts of the monastery; at Woodchester the
novices and their master occupied the first and second (top) floors
of the priory's west wing. The novices shared the refectory and
the sanctuary of the church with the rest of the community, but
otherwise they lived as much apart as possible, having their own
private staircase which gave access to the cloister, and so to the
refectory and church. There were about twenty cells for novices,
and two rooms, a study and a bedroom, for their master. There was
a large common room, for classes and for recreational purposes, an
oratory, with the reserved sacrament, and a bathroom and the usual
offices. The cells were small, rather bleak rooms, with nothing in
them beyond a small table, an upright wooden chair, a bed, and a
washstand. There was no running water, either hot or cold.

The fathers' cells were a little less austere, and usually contained a bookcase that might hold two or three hundred books. In
accordance with Saint Dominic's intentions, the priest-friars were
supposed to be assiduous students of sacred scripture, and of
philosophy and theology, so books were the one item in which a
certain latitude was allowed in respect of possessions; but strictly
speaking, of course, all books belonged to the community, and not
to the individuals whose shelves they graced for the time being.
The laybrothers' cells would contain fewer books, and those mostly
of a devotional nature.

The door of the novitiate was kept locked from the inside,
only the Prior having the right of admission. Other fathers and
brothers had to knock and state their business before they could be
admitted. These 'security' measures were intended to provide the
novices with the maximum of privacy and freedom from disturb-
ance. In fact, even in other parts of the house they were not allowed
to speak with other members of the community unless they had

permission. The purpose of this restriction was, in part, to prevent novices from getting to know 'the secrets of the convent'; as, for instance, its amount and sources of income, or the fact that Father So-and-so had cancer or was an alcoholic. This was a sensible regulation, seeing that novices are free to leave at any time, or can be sent away if they are judged to be unsuitable.

In the novitiate common room there was a small library; it consisted mostly of devotional works and lives of holy Dominicans or other saints. There was no fiction. The novices were not allowed into the conventual library, which was normally kept locked except at such times as the librarian was in attendance. I was once allowed into it on a wet afternoon to give the books, or as many of them as I could, a dusting. The library housed a large and very interesting collection of books, many hundreds of volumes. There were also some manuscripts; among them a collection of letters from the architect A.W. Pugin to Squire William Leigh, the priory's founder. No one seems to know where these letters are now, but in the nineteen sixties I was able to publish their text in the *Aylesford Review*.

Woodchester had the reputation in the Order of being a house of exact and strict observance; and so it was. The brethren rose at 5.30 a.m, and at six o'clock assembled in choir for their morning meditation. At 6.30 there followed the offices of Prime and Terce, before the Conventual Mass, which was sung on festal days. (On Sundays, at eleven o'clock, there was a High Mass with sermon.) Then came breakfast: coffee and bread and butter during the long monastic fast, which lasted from Holy Cross Day, 14th September, until Easter. From Easter until 14th September porridge was served, with milk and golden syrup. In the summer there was not much demand for it; but how welcome it would have been in the winter!

After breakfast we made our beds and tidied our cells before assembling in our common room to listen to a reading from *The Practice of Perfection and Christian Virtues* by Alphonsus Rodriguez, a sixteenth century Spanish Jesuit, which was read from a grotesquely archaic translation which often occasioned more mirth than edification. Later in the morning there were, or were supposed to be, classes in liturgy, the history of the Order, and so on; but as often as not these did not take place. Father Eustace, who was nearing the end of his term of office as novice master, was often unwell, and kept to his room. This was unfortunate for us, for he was an excellent novice master when he was well enough to function. So much so that after he had retired the provincial chapter conferred on him the title of Novice Master Emeritus.

Father Eustace's indisposition left us with a lot of time on our hands in the morning, and with no satisfactory means of filling it. Sebastian Bullough was lucky, for he was helping one of the priests, Father Bruno Walkley, to prepare for publication an English-Latin edition, for congregational use, of the Dominican Missal; so he was kept busy with proof reading and so on.

Anthony Foster (now known as Brother Leander) had been given permission to do a little stone-carving in his spare time, and had brought with him some chisels and a mallet. There were quite a few sizeable pieces of stone lying around outside, left behind, perhaps by the priory's builders, so he had no difficulty in occupying himself. But for me the long, empty mornings were tedious, and hard to get through. There was not really much one could do except look forward to lunch. This was always a good meal; there was no cause for complaint as to the quality or quantity of the simple food provided. The refectory was quite large. The prior and seniors sat at a kind of high table, facing the reader's pulpit in the wall at the opposite end of the room. The rest of the community was seated at refectory tables placed along the length of the room on each side, leaving plenty of space in the middle for the servers to move about in. Only the inner side of each table was occupied, and the seating was strictly in order of seniority.

I used to enjoy the ritual of the refectory. The reading was done by the novices, a week at a time, as was the serving of the meals. The reading was a valuable training for future preachers. If a word were mispronounced, or some other fault occur, such as reading too fast, too loud, too slow, or not loud enough, the father who was the *corrector mensae* stopped the reading, and the word or passage had to be read again, correctly. After three corrections, or only one if made by the Prior, the reader had to make a ritual prostration on the floor after the meal. The same discipline applied to mistakes made when singing or chanting in choir; but here the discipline of the *venia*, as the prostration was called, applied to the fathers and other 'professed' brethren as well as to the novices.

1. Dunheved Castle, from an engraving of 1787

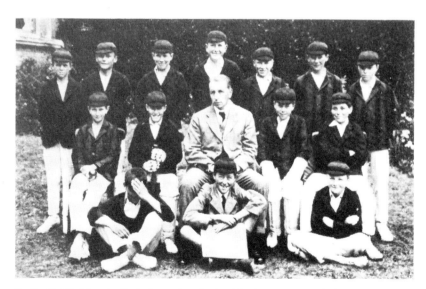

2. E. C. H. Moule (in informal attire) with the Weymouth College Junior School Cricket XI, 1925

3. Guild Chapel and Saint Dominic's Press building: Ditchling Common, 1935. From a drawing by Peter F. Anson.

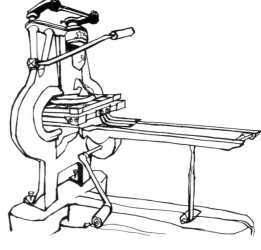

4. The author in RAF battle-dress uniform, 1940

5. Stanhope Press (said to have belonged to William Morris) used by Hilary Pepler at Saint Dominic's Press, Ditchling, 1916-1936 loaned to Saint Albert's Press, Aylesford, 1955-1960. From a drawing by Lesley Pearson.

6. Aylesford Priory

7. At 43 Blenheim Crescent, 1964. (left to right) Oswald Jones, Nicola Wood, Susan Lesley, Jane Percival, Michael Hastings, Frances Horovitz, Michael Horovitz.

8. Henry Williamson at 57 Ladbroke Road, 1965, reading from his work to (left to right) Frances Horovitz, Jane Percival, Alan Fen-Taylor, Michael Horovitz.

9. Brocard Sewell with Ronald Duncan at Morwenstow, 1975.

At Woodchester the novices, but not the fathers or professed laybrothers (i.e. those in solemn vows), wore the monastic tonsure; so once every fortnight our heads were shaved. This was a very uncomfortable proceeding; the discomfort wore off gradually over the next two weeks, and then began all over again. The discomfort was caused in part by the hoods of our capuces. In choir the hood covered one's head during the chanting of the psalms; but at the *Gloria Patri* at the end of each psalm it was pushed back, leaving the head bare. On being pushed back the hood scraped painfully over one's stubbly pate, which was very sensitive. When passing through the cloister one was supposed to have one's head covered – as it was during meals, unless one was serving – but should you encounter one of the brethren walking towards you, you had to push your hood back, as a silent salutation. This too was slightly painful.

On one evening each week a chapter of faults was held in the novitiate common room. (The fathers and laybrothers had their own separate chapters.) The chapter opened with a short talk by the novice master on some aspect of the Rule of Saint Augustine of Hippo, which Dominicans follow, or from the Constitutions of the Order. Next, the father master would draw attention to any slackness in, or breaches of observance that he might have noticed during the past week. Then, standing in front of him, one by one, the novices made public acknowledgment of any faults against the Rule or Constitutions of which they had been guilty during the past week; as, for example, talking or making a noise during the solemn silence at night, misusing or damaging community property, entering another's cell without permission, and so on. The father master would then ask: "Has anyone anything to proclaim against Brother So-and-so?" Usually silence followed; but occasionally someone would say: "I proclaim Brother So-and-so [for such and such a fault]." In conclusion the novice master would admonish the delinquent, and impose on him a small penance. No one ever seemed to bear any malice if he were proclaimed by someone else. The chapter of faults seems now to have disappeared from the life of all religious communities, except perhaps those of Archbishop Lefebvre's 'Petite Église' and the Abbé de Nantes' Contre-Réforme Catholique. This I think is a pity. It seems to me to have been a salutary spiritual exercise, though no doubt it could become, if one were to let it, a matter of routine.

There were some interesting men in the Woodchester community when I was there. The Prior, Fr Robert Bracey, had entered the Order later in life than was then usual, and was a qualified lawyer; but there is some doubt as to whether he had ever actually practised law. He was a Fellow of the Royal Historical Society; some of the many delightful essays on historical subjects that he contributed to *Blackfriars* were reprinted in his book *Eighteenth Century Studies*. He was an authority on the life and works of Dr Johnson; some people thought that he lived more in the eighteenth century than in the twentieth. Fr Godfrey Anstruther, another Dominican historian, used to say that Robert Bracey was the ideal superior for a novitiate house because of the quality of the talks that he gave at the weekly conventual chapter, which was attended by the whole community. (The novices left the chapter room when it was time for the fathers and professed brothers to acknowledge their faults after the Prior's address.)

Fr Ferdinand Valentine was one of the best and best known preachers and retreat conductors in the country. In fact, he was so much in demand that he seemed to spend more time away than at home. When he was in residence his presence was much appreciated by the novices because he always had a smile and a whispered word of encouragement for any novice whom he thought looked discouraged or depressed. Also, he was given to odd and unexpected behaviour of an amusing kind, as when he appeared in choir one day wearing, not the customary leather belt to gird his tunic, but a brightly-coloured dressing-gown cord.

Perhaps the most remarkable member of the community was one of the laybrothers, Reginald Lawson (in religion, Brother David). His father had been a wealthy business entrepreneur. In 1914 or '15 Reginald joined the Army, and at his father's instance applied for a commission. As a result of what followed he had a severe breakdown, and was invalided out. After that, he somehow cast up at Ditchling, where he shared a small cottage with Desmond Chute and David Jones. The name of this humble dwelling was Woodbarton Cottage, but Eric and Mary Gill's three daughters renamed it The Sorrowful Mysteries, not after the 'mysteries' of the rosary, but because they thought the three young men over-serious in their attitude to life.

At Ditchling Reginald Lawson found that he had no real apti-

tude for any of the trades or crafts practised in the Guild of St
Joseph and St Dominic. His next port of call was Quarr Abbey,
on the Isle of Wight, where he was admitted to the Benedictine
community, and remained with the monks for three years. He
seems to have found the life somewhat constricting, in spite of
his being allowed to some extent to 'live out' in the house of a
totally disabled man for whom he felt in some way responsible.
Eventually he left Quarr. After a short spell at Besford Court,
Monsignor Newsome's home in Worcestershire for handicapped
boys, he moved to Oxford, where he got to know the community at
Blackfriars, the Dominican house of studies. There he was greatly
impressed by an old laybrother, John-Dominic Smee (1845-1925),
who had been professed as long ago as 1876. He also admired
another veteran laybrother, Reginald Taylor, and evidently felt that
a way of life that suited them would suit him too. So he offered
himself to the Dominicans as a prospective laybrother, and was
accepted by them as such in spite of his superior education and
intellectual gifts. He gave up much when he finally entered the
cloister. After he had left the Army he had for a time enjoyed a
good income as a film producer.

At Woodchester Brother David was occupied mostly with quite
ordinary domestic duties: cleaning windows, polishing floors, laying the tables in the refectory, and so on. He was a fine musician,
and in the afternoon he would usually spend an hour or so playing
the organ in the church. He died in Rome in 1985, at the age of
ninety-four. He had been living there for a good many years,
latterly at the *convento* of Santa Sabina, on the Aventine, and died,
one may say, in the odour of sanctity.

It is a commonplace that the 'religious life' as experienced from
within is very different from what it is imagined to be like from an
outside view. Like Reginald Lawson at Quarr, I found the life at
Woodchester in some undefinable way constricting, and never felt
at ease there; whereas Sebastian Bullough and some of the others,
though not all, took to the life readily. Possibly I had entered too
soon, before I was psychologically ready for such an experience.
After seven months I decided to leave, though not without regret.
The novice master thought my decision was right.

CHAPTER FIVE

Ditchling

WHEN I left Woodchester I did not want to return to London if I could help it, so I wrote to Hilary Pepler, and he very kindly offered me a job at Saint Dominic's Press. I think he envisaged this as a temporary measure, but in the event I was to stay there for nearly five years. So I went to Ditchling after all. At first I lived with Mr Pepler and his family at Hopkins Crank, an old farmhouse close to the Ditchling Common crossroads. Living conditions at The Crank were spartan by the standards of today. In fact, some people considered them austere even in 1932. In the evenings the house was lit by oil lamps; one went to bed by candle-light. There was no central heating; in the winter the bedrooms were icy. To warm one's bed one took with one a brick heated at the fire in the living room, wrapped up in newspaper. All water was pumped up by hand; there was no running water in the bedrooms. The big, lofty living-room cum dining-room was heated, or was supposed to be, by the fire in a large open fireplace with inglenooks; but most of the heat went up the chimney. In the middle of the room, in which the rafters were exposed, was a large, round dining-room table. In the winter the room was so cold that the household, with any visitors that might be present, often sat round this table wearing hats, greatcoats, and scarves. All this was accepted cheerfully, taken for granted.

At home Hilary was very much the paterfamilias. His wife, Clare Whiteman, who was a little younger than her husband, had a quiet beauty and a gentleness of speech and manner that were a little deceptive. Behind what at times seemed to be a certain vagueness of manner there was a very specific personality; as Hilary sometimes found when he tried to secure her assent to some of his more fanciful schemes and projects. Like him, she came of Quaker stock, and could not at first understand his conversion to Roman Catholicism; she held out for a good while against his attempts to persuade her to join him. Even Fr Vincent McNabb, whose aid was invoked, had no success. In the end she came in of her own accord: when she was ready.

In 1932 Hilary's family was beginning to thin out. David, the eldest son, who had married Eric Gill's daughter Betty, was farming nearby. Stephen, the second son, who had worked in the Press for two years after leaving school, had gone off to become a Dominican, and was now at Hawkesyard Priory, in Staffordshire, following the course of philosophy there. The youngest son, Mark, who was about my own age, was still at home, working in the Press, and intending to make printing his career. The three daughters, Susan, Janet, and Margaret, were still at home.

Earlier, Mr Pepler had been a social worker with the London County Council; in 1916 he left London to set up his printing and publishing enterprise in Ditchling, where Eric Gill, his neighbour in Hammersmith, had settled some years previously. At Ditchling there was a close collaboration between the two men; Gill supplied wood-engravings for Pepler, and Pepler printed and published Gill's early writings. Together they edited *The Game*, the hand-printed magazine reflecting their beliefs and preoccupations, at first in association with the calligrapher Edward Johnston; but Johnston withdrew after the two others had become Catholics.

In 1920 Hilary and Eric, with their families, moved from the village to Ditchling Common, two miles to the north on the Brighton to Crawley road. They had combined to buy land here, on which to build new workshops; first the new brick building to house Saint Dominic's Press, with a section of it allotted to Eric for his stone-carving workshop. They were soon joined by two other craftsmen, George Maxwell, carpenter and builder, from Birmingham, who had been recommended by Fr Vincent McNabb, and Valentine KilBride, a young weaver and dyer from Bradford who had been introduced to the Guild by Fr John O'Connor. The two newcomers were married men, so there were houses as well as workshops to be built. Maxwell built three brick houses, but the new workshops were mostly simple wooden structures, ex-Army huts and the like. The Guild, which was registered for business purposes as The Spoil Bank Association Limited, owned the new houses corporately, except for Maxwell's, which was his own property. The occupants of the other houses paid rent to the Guild, and the same arrangement held good for the workshops. A Statement of Aim for the Guild was drawn up, laying down certain general principles; it stressed also the individual responsibility of each craftsman for maintaining a proper standard of work, and the need to avoid industrial methods of production in general.

In its first years, and for a long time afterwards, the Guild was a specifically Catholic fraternity, and the Guildsmen were required also to be members of the Third Order of Saint Dominic. A small chapel had been built close to the workshops, and there the Guildsmen met twice a day for common prayer of a liturgical kind. This took the form of the psalms and hymns of the Little Office of our Lady, which were sung or chanted from the Dominican rite *Horae Beatae Mariae Virginis*, one of the finest of the Saint Dominic's Press books.

On Ditchling Common the alliance between Pepler and Gill did not last long; their temperaments were too different. In 1924 Gill and his family moved to a disused monastery in the Black Mountains of Brecknockshire, taking with him his assistant Laurence Cribb and his family, Philip Hagreen, painter, wood-engraver, and ivory-carver, and David Jones. Hagreen was later to return to Ditchling.

Hilary was greatly disturbed by Eric's defection, as he regarded it. He never really understood it, and it was a matter of sorrow to him, for he had loved Eric, and had hoped for great things from their association. It was some years before the breach was healed, largely through the quiet influence of Clare Pepler and Mary Gill; but things were never really the same again. How close the two men had once been can be judged from the fact that at a certain point Hilary made a will leaving everything that he had to Eric, to be administered by him in trust for Hilary's children. Hilary held on at Ditchling, for which he won the undying admiration of Fr McNabb. Eventually he parted from the Guild, in pursuit of new interests; but the Guild gained new recruits, and continued in being till 1988, when it was finally wound up.

Hilary Pepler was a man of varied talents and achievements; but his chief claim to remembrance must surely be the magnificent printing done at Saint Dominic's Press. It is incomprehensible that he has received no entry in the *Dictionary of National Biography*, whereas his brother George, knighted for his services to town planning, was thus honoured. But then, DNB's principles of selection have always been mysterious; it contains no entries, for instance, for Cecil Chesterton, Montague Summers, or John Gray. The liturgical printings of Saint Dominic's Press are especially fine, and were much admired by that great typographical authority, Stanley Morison. Outstanding among them is *Cantica Natalia*, a folio of Latin and English Christmas carols with plainchant notation, printed in 36-point Caslon Old Face, for lectern use by choirs. Ninety-five copies only were printed on Batchelor's hand-made paper, in 1926, and bound in brown sail-cloth. And for many years a copy of the quarto *Horae Beatae Mariae Virginis*, with wood-engravings by Eric Gill and Desmond Chute, was on exhibition in the King's Library at the British Museum. But perhaps the most beautiful of the Saint Dominic's Press books is a smaller one: Francis Thompson's long poem *The Mistress of Vision*, with a Commentary by the Reverend John O'Connor. These three books were all printed on handmade paper from the mill of Joseph Batchelor and Son, but *The Mistress of Vision* was printed on a particularly lovely thin handmade paper that Batchelor had made especially for William Morris. Of this paper Pepler had been able to buy the remaining stock.

His printing was not always up to the standard set by these three books. Occasionally it was bad, sometimes of an almost unique badness, due to faulty inking and hurried presswork. The quality of the Ditchling printing was usually at its lowest when the master-printer's spirits were at their lowest. This had been noticeably so just after Gill had left, in 1924, and again in 1928, when his son Stephen, who had been a great support to his father, went to Woodchester.

By the time I joined the Press in 1932 its best days were over, although good work was still being done. The economic conditions of the 1930s were beginning to impose some changes in methods of work. The type was still mostly set by hand, but some of the larger books were now set in Monotype by a firm of commercial type-setters in Bristol, from whom it was hired. Every line of this machine-set type was overrun before printing; that is to say, it was put through the composing stick, and the spacing adjusted by hand. There was nothing wrong with that; but the fact is, the Monotype version of the Caslon Old Face type, the one most used by Saint Dominic's Press, had a slightly 'spindly' quality, which differentiates it, to the trained eye, from type-founders' Caslon.

Another innovation was the installation of a press of the 'Arab' kind, operated by treadle when it was installed, but later by an electric motor. This simple piece of machinery was acquired at the instance of Pepler's partner, Cyril Costick, who had been his first apprentice. Pepler had nothing against a reasonable, controlled use of machinery where it was appropriate, though he much preferred to print by hand. The Arab enabled much larger print-runs to be achieved in a short time; from the point of view of the Press's financial viability this was all to the good. It did not affect the quality of the work done; in fact, one of the most pleasing of the Press's smaller books is the second edition of *The Jesus Psalter*, printed by Costick on the Arab. However, the Arab did not meet with the approval of the other Guildsmen, and in the end it became one of the factors that brought about Pepler's break with the Guild.

Working in Saint Dominic's Press was always enjoyable. When 'the Boss', as his staff called Mr Pepler when he was not present, was away, Mark and Cyril took charge. (In all there were usually five or six workers in the Press; these included Truscott Hargrave, a very efficient young man who was secretary, book-keeper, and packer, and Augustine Linehan, a rather quaint little elderly Irishman, quite a wit in his way, who kept the workshop tidy, helped with odd jobs, and made tea at the appropriate times.)

Work at Saint Dominic's Press was enjoyable. When the Boss was absent we sometimes diversified our work programme with a type battle. For these contests the printer's staff armed themselves with handfuls of type, with which they assailed each other from behind the presses, or other points of vantage. After the contest the type was gathered up off the floor, and distributed back into the cases. Such treatment cannot have been good for it. The marvel was that it was never known for any participant in these type battles ever to be blinded or otherwise injured.

I have sometimes asked other printers if they have ever come across this custom of type battles. The answer has always been no;

it seems to have been a custom peculiar to Saint Dominic's Press. (I do not recommend it.)

In 1928, when I first met Pepler, one of the first things he said to me was: "One needs to have one's religion right, just as one needs to have one's haircut right." He did not enlarge on this, and said nothing more on the matter of religion. He also told me: "Never look back", and I have always found this a useful principle to follow. In 1928 things were still at a fairly low ebb with him. The vexatious process of claim and counter-claim between himself and Eric Gill in the settling up of their joint business affairs was only just completed. Stephen's departure to Woodchester, although his father had approved of it, was a further blow. A letter that he wrote to Stephen (who was by then Brother Conrad) in September 1928, when he went to Woodchester reveals his feelings. After mentioning some of his activities of the moment, Hilary continues:

So are the days not less full than when you knew them. I hope you will write & let me know how you feel. Mother is rather worried about you – fearing that I have forced this step upon you . . . I think it would be well to report fully about your interior view of the life you have chosen. It would be well that your mother should see that you know what you are at and that the thing is no less valuable because you love what you leave behind and are willing to bear the tremendous loss of home in order to do what God requires of you. It is curious what rum notions people have – you would have thought that as you and I have worked side by side in the same shop for two years being in daily fellowship of work & prayer & home that there would have been some sympathy for me in losing my most dear son. It does not seem to strike anyone (except Fr Vincent) that I should miss you more than anyone else could possibly miss you & that your going is as though something inside me were cut out so that I feel as though I were 'not all there' . . . Nevertheless people suffer foolishly if they are making a mistake. We do not want you to do that, and if you have any doubt about the wisdom & rightness of this step – let me know – the way out of Woodchester is as open as the way in – in fact more open.

However, Stephen had no second thoughts, and seems to have been almost a born Dominican.

An outstanding figure on Ditchling Common between the wars was Commander Herbert Shove (his surname being pronounced to

rhyme with Grove), a retired naval officer who lived on his pension
at Hallett's Farm, a small property at the south end of the Common.
The Commander's brother, Gerald Shove, was the well known
Cambridge-Bloomsbury economist who was married to the poet
Fredegond Shove. The Commander was a convert to the Catholic
faith, and had been received into the Church during the war of
1914-1918, when he was in the submarine service. From this he
was invalided out with his health gravely impaired. A further blow
had been the death of his first wife. In the years between the wars
he was a man out of his element; so he was delighted to be recalled
to active service with the Navy in September 1939. In the first war
he had been awarded the DSO; in the second he was promoted
Captain and presented with the OBE. This was for his successful
organization of the defences of the Port of London. He was then
assigned to a special mission on the Gold Coast, where the climate
undermined his health, and he had to be sent back to England,
where he died soon after his return.

Shove was a burly, bearded man; except that he was taller he
looked very much like William Morris. He was a keen Distributist;
at Halletts he farmed in a desultory kind of way, but he was not
suited to the rôle of peasant proprietor. Later he went in for bee-
keeping, and did well at it. During the 1930s he published a book
of Distributist economics, *The Fairy Ring of Commerce*, a critical
analysis of the capitalist-industrialist system. It would be interesting to know what his brother at Cambridge thought of it. Round
about 1935 the Commander took up metal work, and after a few
lessons from Dunstan Pruden began making pewter mugs and other
metal objects in his workshop at Halletts.

Shove was a dogmatic and racy conversationalist, his language
being somewhat nautical in flavour. Although practically tone-deaf,
he took up the study of music, and used to wander over the
Common, in shabby old clothes and a shapeless felt hat, playing
strange airs on a home-made bamboo pipe. One day this led to his
being arrested, by a policeman new to the district, as a vagrant. He
was taken to the police station at Burgess Hill, where he was
quickly identified and released.

Before the era of music and metal-work Shove had run a grocery
shop at Halletts, obtaining his supplies from somewhere in Burgess
Hill and wheeling them back in a small handcart which he had

made from old sugar-crates. Towards the end of the 1930s he declared himself an authority on mysticism and the occult, and took to expounding, Ancient Mariner-like, the works of Saint John of the Cross and the Reverend Montague Summers to anyone he could waylay. Some strange results followed from this; as when a gust of wind blew out his candle while he was constructing a 'microcosmic pentagram' in one of his outbuildings at midnight, and he fled the scene in panic.

Another of the Commander's activities was the operation of an illicit still, the alcohol from which he dispensed to his friends under a variety of flavourings. But the near-destruction of his distillery by fire helped to bring this occupation to an end.

Shove was not the only distiller of contraband liquor on Ditchling Common in those days. Hilary Pepler and George Maxwell made their own spirits, as did Dustan Pruden; and there was at least one other practitioner of the art. The stills were home-made, according to the directions given in an early nineteenth century work of popular instruction, *Dr Lardner's Cabinet Encyclopaedia*, whose volumes could be picked up for a shilling or two in the secondhand-bookshops in The Lanes at Brighton. Inevitably, the existence of these stills eventually became a matter of common knowledge as far afield as Hassocks, where the local customs and excise officer lived. By then it had become too dangerous to continue any longer; so one dark night all the stills were dismantled and buried underneath the turf and bracken of Ditchling Common.

By 1935 the best days of the private press 'movement' were over; most of these enterprises were unable to stand up to the new financial depression, which the then prime minister, Ramsay MacDonald, had described as an economic blizzard. At Saint Dominic's Press Pepler was in conflict with the Guild over the installation of the Arab press, and over his having taken on a non-Catholic boy from the village as an apprentice. He had begun to feel that after twenty years of printing he had had enough; so he decided to close the Press and embark on new activities.

In June 1936 Gilbert Chesterton died, after a short illness. He had been in poor health for some time. Hilary had known Chesterton, and Belloc also, since early in the century, when Hilary had been one of the founders of the Hampshire House Club

for working men in Hammersmith, and had invited Belloc and
Chesterton, and Cecil Chesterton also, to lecture to the working
men. But probably he had met them before this, at meetings of the
Fabian Society. Pepler visited Gilbert Chesterton during his last
illness, and was one of the last people to see him. He had made no
provision for the future of his paper, *G.K.'s Weekly*. Its financial
position was, as always, bad, and it looked as if it would have to
cease publication. In fact, the directors wanted to close it down;
but Pepler was determined that this must not be allowed to happen.
Somehow he managed to persuade the directors to part with it to a
small private group of Distributists, one of whom was Hilaire
Belloc, who agreed to act as editor for the time being.

Hilary's centre of gravity now moved to London, though his
home was still at Hopkins Crank. New and larger offices, in
Essex Street, were taken for *G.K.'s Weekly*, which was renamed *The
Weekly Review*. Two secretaries were installed, and the day to day
running of the paper was looked after by Pepler and Belloc's
son-in-law Reginald Jebb. At first Belloc came up to the office
once a week; but he relinquished the editorship as soon as he
could, and passed it over to Rex Jebb, while continuing himself to
contribute regular articles, mostly on foreign affairs. Pepler had
also taken on the secretaryship, unpaid, of the Distributist League,
and needed an assistant who would be able to travel to speak at
meetings in different parts of the country. The post was offered to
me. How he did it I don't know, but he managed to raise the
necessary funds to pay me a modest salary. I enjoyed the work,
which took me to various places, most of them in the Midlands,
where the Distributist movement had its main strength: among
them Birmingham, Leicester, and Derby.

So now I was back more or less where I had started in 1928; but
with the difference, that predictions of the inevitability of war with
Germany made the future seem very uncertain. Another part of my
job was to help Pepler with his work for the Distributist League in
London. Towards the end of 1936 I got him to approve the idea of a
public debate between a Distributist and a Communist, each to be
a well known public figure. Fr McNabb agreed to appear for the
Distributists, and the Communist Party of Great Britain put forward
as their representative John Strachey, the future Labour Party
cabinet minister. In the course of arranging this event I had a

number of meetings, at the Communist headquarters in Covent Garden, with Emil Burns, a young man not much older than myself, who had been educated at Ampleforth. After his senior, R. Palme Dutt, Emil Burns was the leading intellectual of the Community Party of Great Britain. I have often wondered what became of him. Today's CPGB – I believe it is in the process of changing its name – seems to have no thinkers or writers of this calibre. But at least it is still, though perhaps tenuously, in being; whereas the Distributist League and movement have vanished without trace.

The debate took place on 17th February, 1937 in the small hall at the Central Hall, Westminster. The small hall holds about four hundred people; on the night, far more than that number turned up. In fact, the hall was uncomfortably crowded, and a lot of people had to stand. Rather to my surprise there seemed to be in the audience more Communists and Socialists than Distributists and Catholics; but whereas the Communist Party had been able to advertise the event in the *Daily Worker*, the Distributists had only *G.K.'s Weekly*, with its small circulation.

The debate was reported at length in the next morning's *Daily Express* and *Manchester Guardian*. This seems to have been the last occasion when Distributism was treated as a live issue in the national press. The *Daily Express* said that two brilliant men had spent two and a half hours at cross purposes. 'It was a called a debate . . . It was highly entertaining.' Later, the Distributist League published a verbatim report under the title *Communism versus Distributism*.

Father McNabb rarely refused an invitation to debate. He was a brilliant and attention-holding speaker, and always attracted a large audience. A few months after the debate with John Strachey he accepted a challenge from the Protestant Truth Society to debate a motion to the effect that the English Roman Catholic martyrs of the sixteenth and seventeenth centuries were traitors who had been justly executed for treason. This debate was held in the Caxton Hall, Westminster, which was packed with Catholics and Protestants in roughly equal proportions. They had been issued with tickets of one colour for Catholics and another colour for Protestants, so that they could be directed to seats on opposite sides of the hall. Presumably a breach of the peace was feared unless they were kept apart. There were two chairmen, the one Protestant, Sir

Alfred Baker, a solicitor; the other, Mr Richard O'Sullivan, KC, a Catholic. The debate was opened by the Protestant speaker, Mr Alfred Close, as to whose profession or occupation nothing was disclosed. This debate was yet another instance of two speakers being at cross purposes. Fr McNabb took the term 'Roman Catholic martyrs' to mean men or women who had been beatified or canonized as martyrs, or who had at least been declared Venerable because they had died for their religion. Mr Close understood by the term any Roman Catholic who had been sentenced to death under the penal laws against Catholics. Mr Close supported his case with a series of lantern-slides of popes, cardinals, Jesuits (such as Fr Robert Persons), and others who had authorized, or at least encouraged, plots to assassinate Queen Elizabeth; but none of those whom he named was ranked by the Church as a martyr.

When Mr Close had finished putting his case, complete deadlock followed. Fr McNabb sat down, and refused to respond to his opponent's indictment until his own interpretation of the terms of the debate was ruled to be correct. Eventually, after an interval, the two chairmen ruled in his favour; but during this hold-up in the proceedings the audience became very restive and noisy; the Protestants rather more so than the Catholics. It was undoubtedly a good thing that the two parties had been seated on opposite sides of the hall. In the end, order was restored, and the debate proceeded, to end on a relatively harmonious note with the singing of the National Anthem.

In the late 1930s there were many interesting political meetings in London. I heard several fine left-wing speakers: among them the veteran Trades Union leader Tom Mann, the then general secretary of the Communist Party, Harry Pollitt, and Conrad Noel, the Anglo-Catholic Communist vicar of Thaxted: all of them impassioned orators. But by far the greatest orator of those times was a politician supposedly of the Right, Sir Oswald Mosley. In the late thirties Mosley was attracting huge audiences with his policies for restoring Britain's greatness, and putting an end to the corruption and inefficiency of the old Party System, and keeping Britain out of another fratricidal European war. After the war, which he had failed to prevent, when he had retired from politics, I got to know Mosley quite well, and found him to be a man of wide culture and great humanity. I never heard him say in private a harsh word about any of his political opponents, in spite of his three and a half years' imprisonment without trial, no charges of any offence having been brought against him. His 'crime', a new one in Britain, had been simply that of trying to prevent the outbreak of a new war in 1939, and continuing to advocate a peaceful negotiated settlement after it had broken out.

Towards the end of 1937 I got to know another remarkable man, of quite different character: Brother Joseph Gard'ner, impresario, actor, educationalist, circus proprietor, and founder of a religious order. But I shall not write of him here since an account of his strange career will be found in my biography *Cancel All Our Vows*, published in 1988.

1937 was a disturbing time. War was already in the air, and neither the Distributist League nor the *Weekly Review* seemed likely to have an assured future. And it could only be a matter of time before I was called up for military service; so when I received from my friend Edward Walters an invitation to help him in his private press at Primrose Hill, in north-west London, I was quite happy to accept. Edward Walters was born in 1899, and was an Oxford graduate. He had learned printing and wood-engraving at the Central School of Arts and Crafts, and in 1929 he had set up his own press in the attic of his parents' house, 36 Oppidans Road, NW3. This was always more or less a one man enterprise; Walters printed, illustrated, and bound his books himself; but sometimes when he had an exceptionally heavy load of work he would take on a temporary assistant. He had a large and a small Albion press, an Adana bench-model press for letterheads, visiting cards, and such-like small items, and used exclusively Caslon Old Face type from the firm of Stephenson, Blake, successors to the Caslon foundry. He produced a number of small poetry reprints: Gray's 'Elegy', Crashaw's *Musicks Duell*, with wood engravings by Philip Hagreen, Patmore's *A Child's Purchase*, and two small anthologies of his favourite poems, illustrated from his own wood blocks, together with some original works; among them his own poem *Silva Civica*, on the history and beauties of Hampstead Heath, and, a much larger book, *The English Antiquaries*, by his father, H.B. Walters, FSA. Walters was a patient and careful craftsman; some good judges considered him a better printer than Hilary Pepler. Whereas Pepler liked to 'get a move on' in the workshop, Walters was prepared to spend any amount of time 'making ready'. His books have a particular charm. He never sought publicity, and his work is still relatively little known. He was a tall, handsome man, with silver hair, and a quirky sense of humour. Working with him was always enjoyable.

What Walters wanted me to help him with was the setting up and printing of a fine edition, on handmade paper, of *The Quest of the Sangraal*, the long blank-verse poem by Robert Stephen Hawker (1803-1875), the famous Vicar of Morwenstow. The book was to be embellished with wood-engravings by Philip Hagreen. Unhappily, the rapid approach of war brought this project to an end half-way through. A number of sheets, amounting to about half the poem, had been printed, and then Walters was forced to close down the Press, and to evacuate himself and his aged parents to Somerset. On the outbreak of war the house in Oppidans Road was requisitioned for occupation by refugees from the Continent. Walters was too old for active service – he had been in the Navy for a short time towards the end of the previous war – and got himself appointed to a teaching post at Marlborough School. When he returned to Oppidans Road after the war he found that the attic workshop had been damaged by a flying bomb aimed at nearby St Pancras station. Fortunately, all the type-cases and presses had been removed to Marlborough; but of the printed sheets of Hawker's *Quest* no trace remained. Nor of Hagreen's wood-blocks. The galleys and formes holding the type of the remainder of the book had also vanished. Sadly, work on the book was never resumed.

During the time that I was with Walters we started a quarterly magazine, *The Thing*, of which only one number ever appeared. It was an eight-page quarto, set up and printed by hand. There were two editions, or states: one on handmade paper, the other, priced more cheaply, on machine paper. The contents included an article by the mathematician-craftsman Romney Green on his experience of teaching woodwork to the unemployed, and one by myself on Hawker, for which Walters supplied a fine wood-engraving, after an old photograph of the poet. I had secured promises of future contributions to the magazine from Arthur Machen, Montague Summers, and Eric Gill; but no further numbers appeared. I believe we enlisted about fifty subscribers from among our friends and others, and printed about two hundred copies all told. The unsold copies all seem to have disappeared: some in the blitz, perhaps? So that the magazine is now, to use a phrase that Montague Summers was fond of, of the last rarity. In fact, I have no copy myself.

CHAPTER SIX

R.A.F.

EARLY in 1939 everyone within a certain age-span had to register for military service. I did not at all want to be incorporated into the Army, and I was pretty sure I would not be accepted by the Navy; so I expressed a preference, as one was allowed to, for the Royal Air Force. While waiting for my call-up papers I had two successive temporary jobs: one teaching at a prep school in Tring, Hertfordshire, which I rather enjoyed, the other with the Hague and Gill Press in High Wycombe. This press had been started by Eric Gill in 1930 at Pigotts, his hilltop home a few miles out of High Wycombe. Part of his purpose in setting up this printing office had been to provide his son-in-law René Hague (Ampleforth and Oxford, but undegree'd) with a means of support for himself and his family. Hague was one of the cleverest men I have ever known, and one of the most scholarly, in his unique and unorthodox way. Of Irish origin, he was an independent spirit if ever there was one, and a wonderfully entertaining conversationalist. His very special personality has been successfully captured by Barbara Wall in her *René Hague: A Personal Memoir*, published in 1989. One could never have pictured René in any ordinary employment. He had been sacked from his job with George Coldwell, the London dealer in secondhand Catholic books, and he was sacked from Robert Gibbings's Golden Cockerel Press, where he learned the craft of printing. In the meantime he had married Eric and Mary's youngest daughter. The special quality of the partnership between René and Joan comes across very well in the book that René edited, *Dai Greatcoat: a self-portrait of David Jones in his letters*.

To begin with, the Hague and Gill Press was a very small affair, with a folio Albion handpress and a powered machine of the 'platen' variety called an Autovic. The type was set by hand, and in its early years the Press had the exclusive use of Eric Gill's Joanna typeface, named after his daughter. Gradually the Press expanded, taking on more and more outside work, until eventually it formed some kind of business association with Dent's, the London publishers. It was then moved from Pigotts to larger premises in High Wycombe, and modern machinery was installed.

While I was working at the Press in High Wycombe I was living at Pigotts. I shall not say much here about Eric Gill: four biographies of him have been written, all of which have their merits; but the best, and most recent, is that by Fiona MacCarthy, and not only because she was the first to make full use of Gill's private diaries. It would seem that in some way I helped to set her on the path that led to her becoming his biographer. In 1965, when she was a young feature writer on *The Guardian*, and already an authority on design, Fiona made some allusion in her column to the guild of Catholic craftsmen at Ditchling. Something that she said seemed to me not quite accurate, and I wrote to ask her about it. The result of this was that a little later we spent a day at Ditchling. We had lunch with Valentine KilBride, the weaver, and his wife Cecilia, and were able to visit all the workshops. A good many years later, in the early 1980s, when I was stationed at Whitefriars School, Cheltenham, I was able to accompany Fiona and her son Corin on a day's excursion to Capel-y-ffin, where Gill had lived from 1924-'28. Her life of Eric Gill has perhaps somewhat eclipsed her *Life in the Country*, a study of C.R. Ashbee and his Guild of Handicraft at Chipping Camden: a book that is equally worth reading. I look forward to her forthcoming life of William Morris.

One may perhaps wonder why Gill's diaries were not destroyed by the family after his death, or at least why they were made available for public inspection so soon. But Eric was a notably truthful man. ('Veritas' is the motto of the Dominican Order, of which he was a tertiary). During his lifetime he was regarded by many as a model Catholic layman, and this, for he was in some ways a very humble man, must have irked him. The diaries are the rebuttal of this false image of himself that he could not refute in his lifetime. I do not know how one reconciles his rampantly dis-ordered sexuality with his profession of adherence to the Christian moral code; probably it is not possible to do so. But I am quite sure that there was nothing of the hypocrite about him. He was a very good friend to me when I was starting out in life. I still remember him as a holy man, which was the considered opinion of his parish priest, the late Father Lockyer, of High Wycombe.

Life at Pigotts was ordered differently from life at Ditchling. Pigotts was essentially a family affair, or rather, an extended family affair, with something of a patriarchal flavour. Eric and Mary lived in the big house, the old farm house, with its wisteria-covered roof. There was a resident chaplain, at first Dom Bernard McElligott, a monk of Ampleforth, who was succeeded by Dr Patrick Flood, a retired seminary professor from the diocese of Glasgow. There was a small chapel in the house, where Eric served the Mass (that is, assisted the priest) every morning before breakfast. His stone-carving workshop was in an old barn immediately adjacent to the house. He usually had three or four assistants; chief among them at this time were Laurence Cribb and Anthony Foster. In separate cottages close by were René and Joan Hague and their children, and Denis Tegetmeier, painter and engraver, his wife Petra Gill, and their children.

A very entertaining and by no means inaccurate fictionalized account of life at Pigotts will be found in Elizabeth Taylor's novel *The Wedding Group*; but it must be emphasized that if the 'Quayne' of the novel is recognizably Pigotts, Harry Bretton, the painter, and patriarch of Quayne, is nothing like Eric Gill.

On 3rd September, 1939 Britain declared war on Germany. Memory can be very deceiving, as I often find now in my eightieth year. I have a clear recollection of prime minister Neville Chamberlain's broadcast to the nation; but I cannot have heard it when it was delivered, because on that bright Sunday morning I was cycling from Tring to Pigotts to have lunch with Eric and Mary. I must have heard the broadcast when it was repeated later in the day. I was saddened and disturbed by the outbreak of war: that war which the chief survivors of what Henry Williamson called 'the phoenix generation', the Prince of Wales (later King Edward VIII and Duke of Windsor), Lawrence of Arabia, Major-General J.F.C. Fuller, Sir Oswald Mosley, and Henry Williamson himself had warned against, and done what they could to prevent. So had other distinguished people, representative of other points of view: among them Dick Sheppard, then Dean of Saint Paul's, and Eric Gill, both of whom were opposed not only to this war, but to all wars. I myself was a member of PAX, a society of Catholic pacifists and other war resisters, of which Eric Gill, I think, was the president. Certainly he and Donald Attwater, and the philosopher E.I. Watkin, were among its more prominent members. However, while admiring and approving the stand made by conscientious objectors, I felt that for me there would be something wrong if I were to opt out from the common ordeal facing one's friends and fellow-countrymen.

In April 1941 my call-up papers arrived, and soon afterwards I joined a large group of new entrants at the RAF station at Padgate, a dreary suburb of Warrington, in Lancashire. At Padgate we were kitted out with our uniforms and equipment, and sent off to Blackpool for our initial training. There we spent hours every day drilling in the huge Amusements Park, which was closed to the public. It was hard going; but I found it unexpectedly enjoyable, even though we were a scratch lot of amateur potential soldiers, with, it seemed, very little aptitude for the martial arts.

The morning and afternoon drill sessions were often broken by a lecture, usually either boring or faintly comic, on some aspect of military science; it might be the correct use of gas-masks, the psychology of the enemy (whom most of our instructors had never set eyes on, and with whose country and language they were not familiar), the spirit of the RAF, and so on. Our NCOs, corporals for the most part, seemed as much wearied by these lectures as we were; probably more so, for they must have listened to them countless times, and so were glad enough when a lecture was over to march us off down some side street for a cup of tea and a smoke in one of the town's numerous small cafés.

Our martial progress was slow. We did not take readily either to foot drill or arms drill. As the days passed, our instructors' patience grew less, and their language stronger. Their job must have been very tedious. They had to turn out, in the shortest possible time, squads of properly trained airmen; but we had not the temperament of the 'regular' soldier, and obstinately remained civilians in uniform. Eventually, however, we emerged from the obscurity of the Amusements Park, and were drilled on the promenade, in full view of the public. Things went no better there. Perhaps we were embarrassed by the presence of spectators; or perhaps we were just exhausted. We were all ineptitude and incapacity.

Corporals, sergeants, and flight-sergeants could do nothing with us. Then, one morning, there was a surprise. There appeared on the sea-wall, which we were facing, the Station Warrant Officer, Mr Pope, who told us that as we were so backward he proposed to take us in hand himself. This was scarcely welcome news, since the SWO of any RAF station was usually a tough old veteran with a loud voice and a rough tongue.

However, Warrant Officer Pope was not of this kind. He was youngish, very smart in appearance, very correct and alert in his bearing, and brisk in his movements. He had infinite patience, gave his orders clearly, without shouting, and never used coarse language; nor was he other than polite to the men he was drilling. What a change from our previous instructors. We made rapid progress, and quite soon became proficient in the ceremonial drill that would be required of us at our 'passing out' parade.

After we had passed out we were posted to RAF units in different parts of the country. I was sent, by myself, to Number 22 Operational Training Unit at Wellesbourne Mountford, near Stratford-on-Avon. This was a Bomber Command station, part of Eight Group, whose headquarters were at Abingdon. The Unit's function was to train air crew – pilots, navigators, and rear-gunner bomb-aimers – for Wellington aircraft. Wellesbourne was a temporary airfield, on some of the best agricultural land in Warwickshire.

At Blackpool most of the recruits had taken tests that qualified them for specialist training – very few were of the physical standard required for air crew – as fitters, riggers, radio operators, drivers, mechanics, clerks, medical orderlies, etc. I had wanted to qualify for training as a Special Duties Clerk (Clerk/SD), which I had heard was an interesting job; but I failed to pass a simple test in mathematics, and so had to remain, at least for the time being, a lowly ACH/GD (Aircrafthand General Duties). The ACHs did most of the rougher and more menial work on the camp, such as cleaning out the latrines and doing odd jobs in the cookhouse. But there was one advantage; some of these lowly duties were done without any supervision, so that often the ACH could knock off from his work quite early in the afternoon, while his more skilled colleagues had to labour on until five or even six p.m. Before long, though, someone told me that I might be able to get accepted as an Acting Clerk/SD, with the trade test indefinitely deferred if I were able to do the work efficiently. It seemed worth a try. There was at the moment a shortage of Clerks/SD at Wellesbourne, so I was able to get taken on without much difficulty.

Special Duty clerks worked mostly in Flying Control towers and in Operations Rooms, plotting the movements of aircraft, coding and decoding messages in cipher, and so on. This was responsible work; among other things it involved decoding the signals from Group HQ that gave the secret recognition letters and colours of the day to be flashed by home-coming night-flying aircraft; and also the letters of the day to be flashed by the mobile aerial lighthouse that was stationed somewhere in the countryside not far from our airfield. In big operations rooms most of the SD clerks were WAAFs (members of the Women's Auxiliary Air Force), who were particularly good at work of this kind. At Wellesbourne, a non-operational station, the ops room was quite small, and was manned by three or four officers and four or five airmen, working in shifts around the clock.

The Senior Operations Officer, Flight-Lieutenant Waller, was an elderly 'dugout' from the previous war, in which he had served as a Major – a title by which he was still sometimes addressed – in the Royal Flying Corps. He was a man of private means, and owned a large milling business in Rathkeale, Co. Limerick. A typical Anglo-Irish gentleman of the Ascendancy, he enjoyed shooting, fishing, and other country pursuits, which he was able to follow in the Warwickshire countryside when he was off duty. He was easy to work for, friendly and considerate to his staff. Intellectually he was not brilliant, and a certain proneness to muddle showed that he might be older than he looked. How it was that the Operations Room at Wellesbourne Mountford was not reduced to chaos under his amiable direction it would be hard to say. His clerks always said that without their help he would soon bring the whole flying-training programme to a standstill. But servicemen always talk about their officers like that; in spite of his air of bluff confusion and bewilderment Mr Waller probably had more control over what was going on than we affected to believe.

Wellesbourne was a pleasant camp. I was billeted in a hut full of clerks of various kinds, and we lived together harmoniously. We rarely had to attend parades or go on guard duty. I do not remember that we ever had firing practice with our rifles, but occasionally we had hand-grenade practice on a range in nearby Eckington Woods. I never enjoyed this. It was always a nasty moment when you pulled out the pin that kept the grenade safe, so that then there was only your finger holding down the safety catch. It was still more alarming when you threw the grenade; I always had the feeling that it was sure to fall short and blow one up. It was always a relief when the ordeal was over.

In the daytime on this Warwickshire airfield the war seemed quite remote; but at night, when the Luftwaffe was droning overhead, on its way to attack industrial targets in the Midlands, it seemed much too close. During these night-time alerts our own night-flying programme had to stop. The flarepath on our runway was put out, and the dummy flarepath in a field a few miles away was switched on, in the hope of deceiving the enemy. Only one bomb ever fell on the airfield at Wellesbourne when I was there, and that was probably an accident. It destroyed an empty stationary aircraft standing at a dispersal point, but hurt no one. On another night a German plane followed one of our aircraft home, and tried to shoot it up as it was landing; but without success. The German plane then made off, unharmed. During night-flying exercises, inevitably, and even occasionally in the daytime, there were a number of fatal crashes of aircraft flown by pilots who were still under training. Usually the whole crew would be killed. There was one dreadful winter night when a snowstorm which had not been forecast by our Met. Office suddenly came on; five aircraft crashed while trying to land.

Wellington aircraft were very cumbersome machines. Now and then we were called upon by Group Headquarters to help make up the number of planes needed for some extra-large night-time operation over Germany. This meant sending into action aircrews that were not properly trained, with pilots who had never flown over Germany before. The first time we had to do this was on the occasion of the first one-thousand-bomber raid on Cologne. The atmosphere in the Operations Room that evening was very tense. The captains and crews of the aircraft had been called to the Ops Room, and in their presence the secret orders for the day were handed by Mr Waller to the Station Commander, a Group Captain and former pilot, for him to open, and then read out the contents. The orders began with the words: 'Object of the mission: To

DESTROY COLOGNE.' This was the beginning of Winston Churchill's policy of terror-bombing, by which he hoped to break the morale of the German civilian population. Of course, it failed; just as the Luftwaffe's retaliatory bombing of London and other big cities failed.

On the night of the Cologne raid RAF Wellesbourne Mountford lost several aircraft, with their crews. This was not surprising, since most of the men involved had had no previous operational experience. A sad part of it was that for 'security' reasons the aircrews were confined on that evening to their barracks or to the sergeants' mess, so that their girlfriends were not able to see them before they took off.

After a year or so at Wellesbourne I was transferred to our 'satellite' airfield at Gaydon, near Banbury. At Gaydon I worked in Flying Control, and my duties were much the same as they had been at Wellesbourne. At Gaydon we had a WAAF w/t (radio) operator, which gave the control room a note of civility. Gaydon is on the Warwick to Banbury road, which was good for hitching lifts from passing cars. A serviceman or woman in uniform was seldom refused. The longest lift I ever had, from a young woman, seemingly a civilian, of singular beauty, was from Gaydon to Croydon. Probably I was on my way to visit Hilary and Clare Pepler at Ditchling.

In the control room we worked for eighteen hours on and thirty-six off. In our off time we were free to leave the camp, as long as we had obtained the necessary pass. On our single days off one went to Leamington Spa rather than to Stratford-on-Avon. In Stratford everything, including the simplest of meals in cafés, was exorbitantly expensive. One reason why I wish it could be proved beyond doubt that the works attributed to the man of Stratford, William Shakespeare, were written by Francis Bacon, Viscount St Alban's – or by anyone else – is that it would deprive Stratford of its tourist trade, and thus put an end to the impudence of the burghers in extracting from gullible Americans and others large sums of money for admission to the so-called 'Birthplace'. This house, which has a yearly 'gate' as big as the Cup Final's, was not acquired by Shakespeare *père* until eleven years after the birth of his son William. The real birthplace was burned down over a hundred years ago.

Sometimes I used to cycle from Gaydon to the village of Chacombe, in Northamptonshire, just the other side of Banbury, to visit a delightful family called Welford, to whom a friend had introduced me. In Chacombe I met again, after an interval of twenty years, my step-grandmother, Agnes Grylls. To the amazement of everyone in Launceston, my grandfather had died virtually bankrupt, and had left her unprovided for. How this came about is something of a mystery. I remember that there was a framed photograph of Monte Carlo in his smoking-room at Trenuth; I should think it likely that he had made some unlucky financial speculations, which perhaps he had attempted to redress by gambling. The second Mrs Grylls was now employed as companion to the Dowager Duchess of Marlborough, a very 'difficult' old lady, as Mrs Welford told me, who had come to live at Chacombe. I was rather nervous at the prospect of meeting Agnes Grylls again, since as a child I had resented her installation at Trenuth, and had made life difficult for her. Fortunately, when we met again we quickly made friends, and old strifes, already mostly forgotten, were forgiven.

While I was stationed at Gaydon, Operation Sea Lion, the German invasion of England, was imminently expected. It had been given out by the Government that the signal that the invasion had begun would be the ringing of all the church bells in the country, which had been silent since the beginning of the war. One night, when I was on duty in the Control Tower, we heard the Gaydon church bells pealing out, and those of the neighbouring village, Kineton, also; but it was a false alarm. Or so it was announced the next day. It seems certain that Operation Sea Lion was never launched, but there are reasons to think that the Germans had mounted some kind of dress rehearsal for it, which was not a success.

After two years of this pleasant but unexciting life at Gaydon and Wellesbourne I applied for a change, and was soon afterwards posted to the Coastal Command station at Stornoway, in the Outer Hebrides. RAF Stornoway was responsible for the control of military aircraft being ferried from the United States to Britain. After leaving Iceland, the next stop for these planes was Stornoway, from where they went on to Prestwick. The control tower at Stornoway was manned jointly by RAF and United States Army Air

Force officers and men. Working conditions were pleasant, but a good deal more demanding than at Gaydon. Often there would be as many as fifty planes circling the airfield, at different heights, awaiting permission to land. To get them all safely down was the responsibility of the duty officer and his assistants. During the few months that I was there there were no accidents; and I never heard that there had been any previously.

Outside working hours – and again one was working all round the clock, in shifts – life at Stornoway was dull. There was nowhere to go when one was off duty; the little town had nothing to offer, and the island's historic and prehistoric monuments were too far away to be reached easily. It seemed to rain for six days out of seven, and the rain was heavier than any I had seen in England. The wind was often so strong that when it was in a certain direction it would take half an hour or more to walk against it the hundred or so yards from the airfield to our billets. These Nissen huts had been known to be uprooted from their concrete bases, to which they were anchored by wire cables, and blown into the sea. And yet, on fine days, with no wind, no rain, blue skies, and bright sunshine, it was a paradisal place.

After about three months at Stornoway I was so bored that I responded to an appeal in the DROs (Daily Routine Orders) for volunteers to train as Maps Clerks (Clerks G/D Maps), which would mean a posting back to the mainland. I realized that some knowledge of mathematics would be required for the theoretical part of this course, but that was a hurdle that could be either jumped over or fallen down at when the time came. Maps Clerks were trained at Bentley Priory, the headquarters of RAF Fighter Command, in Stanmore, Middlesex, and also of the United States Army Air Force in Britain. In charge of the Maps Section was a British Army officer, Major Godfrey, and an American officer, Major Bernier, who were assisted by a very able WAAF, Section Officer Joan Girling, and by two or three clerks.

The course of training for Maps Clerks was supposed to comprise six months' practical work in the Map Store, to be followed by a six months' course in cartographical theory.

The Map Store was in two parts: one in a Nissen hut at Bentley Priory, the other in a requisitioned shop in Bushey High Street, a quarter of a mile away. There were three or four other trainees, all agreeable men. We spent most of our time packing up huge parcels of aerial maps of different parts of Germany, for despatch to RAF units on the Continent. Humping heavy piles of very large maps from the racks on which they were stacked onto the packing tables was tiring work; but it did familiarize us, as it was intended to do, with the different maps and the code letters and numbers by which they were identified. Tea was always brewing and smoking was allowed, so the time passed quite pleasantly.

After three or four months I was transferred to the subsidiary map store in Bushey High Street. At the Priory our immediate superior was one Corporal Vaizey, who in private life had worked in a bank; in Bushey High Street a civil servant, Mr Charles Fardell, was in charge. He was a sociable man, easy and pleasant to work with and for. In the High Street we used to go out for our cups of tea to a café across the road which was patronized by Army and ATS personnel also.

In the Maps Section we rarely saw our officers; we seemed to be exempt from parades and guard duties, at least none came our way, and there was a minimum of military formality. Nor was there any weapons-training. I was billeted in a hut in the grounds of Bentley Priory, where we drank mugs-full of steaming hot tea before we got up in the morning. The secret of this sybaritic existence was that in our hut we had three or four good-natured men who worked in the cookhouse. They had to get up early each morning, before the rest of us, and were so kind as to bring over to our hut a large bucketful of tea, from which we filled our mugs.

Apart from the Luftwaffe's air raids life went on smoothly enough. These bombing raids were a great nuisance, especially at night. At first when the sirens sounded we used to tumble out of our bunks, grab what clothing we could, and a blanket or two, and dive for the underground shelters. But these were so cold and unpleasant that before long most of us preferred to stay in our bunks and take a chance. The drone of the approaching German aircraft – a quite different sound from that made by our own planes – always inspired fear, and the noise from the anti-aircraft gunfire and falling bombs was even more unnerving.

Gradually the Luftwaffe's visits became less frequent; but then came the horror of Hitler's 'secret weapons', the V1 flying bomb, or doodlebug, and the V2 rocket. The flying bombs usually came singly, and looked like a kind of miniature aircraft; at night one could see the red flame of their exhaust. They had a peculiarly threatening drone, which grew louder and louder as they got nearer. The danger-point was when the engine cut out and the machine began its silent descent. This was always a most anxious and fearful moment; but when you heard the explosion, which was often uncomfortably near at hand, you knew you were safe.

The rockets were even more devastating in the damage they could do; but they were invisible, and, until you heard the explosion, inaudible. They inflicted terrible damage and loss of life. If Hitler had had more of these weapons, and had been able to deploy them earlier, Britain would have had to capitulate. The first person who gave the public any warning of the V2s was Sir Oswald Mosley, in his paper *Action*, in the early days of the war. (Soon afterwards *Action* was suppressed by the Government.) It is not known that the Government took any notice of his warning; if it did, he certainly received no thanks for it. It was a good while before the RAF was ordered to begin attacking the launching-pads across the Channel.

As time went on, the trainee Map Clerks who were at Bentley Priory when I arrived there completed their courses and left, and were replaced by newcomer trainees. I had been there a full year, and still nothing had been said about my course in the theoretical aspect of cartography. Then, one morning, I was told that Major Godfrey wanted to see me. I went over to his office, and he told me that he had received a signal from Air Ministry instructing him to supply at once a fully trained Maps Clerk for an urgent overseas posting. Since I was the only unmarried man on the strength, it would have to be me. I must take my trade test as soon as possible. I was sent off to get various injections and inoculations, from which it was surmised that I was probably destined for somewhere in the Far East. And I was told that I would have to take my trade test in forty-eight hours' time. On passing it, I would at once be promoted to the rank of Leading Aircraftman, with an increase in my rate of pay.

I did not see how I could hope to prepare myself in two days for an examination that normally took six months of concentrated study to prepare for; but, of course, I could not have passed it even if I had studied for six years. To make things yet more awkward,

Major Godfrey told me, with suitable apologies, that neither himself nor Major Bernier nor Miss Girling could spare the time to coach me. The best he could do would be to lend me an empty office to study in, and some suitable textbooks.

To fail the exam was out of the question. I had some reputation with my superiors and colleagues for education and intelligence; were I to fail the trade test they would conclude that I had flunked it on purpose, to get out of an unpleasant posting. What was to be done?

As I saw it, there was really only one course open to me, and it depended on the doubtful possibility of being left to do my trade test on my own, with no supervisor or invigilator. On the evening before the fateful day I walked over to the Map Store after hours, and took away, unnoticed, a copy of the RAF Map Catalogue, and a few books on the history and science of map-making.

The next morning – happily it was still winter – I stuffed all these items into the capacious pockets of my service greatcoat, and went along to report to Major Godfrey. To my great relief he explained that all three officers were too busy to look after me, and directed me into the same small office I had used on the day before, handed me the printed examination questions, and left me alone to get on with it. There was hardly a single question to which I knew the answer; but there were no interruptions, and with the help of the various manuals I had smuggled in I managed to do a very creditable paper.

The next day I was told that I had passed my trade test, and could now wear on my sleeve the badge of a Leading Aircraftman. An hour later a signal was received from Air Ministry cancelling my posting.

I have never felt any misgivings over the ethics of this action. For one thing, the exam had been unfairly thrust upon me – which was not at all Major Godfrey's fault – allowing me almost no time for preparation. (The fact that no adequate preparation would have been possible in any amount of time makes no difference.) For another, to have failed it would have been construed as an act of cowardice on my part. Thirdly, there were no other candidates, so no one suffered. The welcome pay increase that now came to me had been earned by a year and more of hard work.

Soon afterwards I was posted to an RAF Disarmament Unit which was being formed at Kenley, in Surrey. In the event I was never required to demonstrate my knowledge of cartographical theory. There was never any need for it.

The purpose of disarmament units was to occupy captured airfields in Germany, and to use them as bases for the inspection of all factories and workshops within a certain area, so as to make sure that no weapons or other military *matériel* were being manufactured clandestinely.

In April 1945 our unit crossed the Channel from Folkestone to Boulogne in tank-landing craft. We quite expected to be attacked by the Luftwaffe or by German submarines; but there was no sign of either. We had a very smooth crossing, and spent the night at Saint Omer, a place associated in my mind with the English Jesuit college founded there in the sixteenth century by the famous Fr Robert Persons; whose name, incidentally, is pronounced Parsons. Like Samuel Taylor Coleridge, he was born at Nether Stowey, in the county of Somerset; but when I visited Nether Stowey a few years ago I could find no one there who had so much as heard of Persons. S.T.C., whose little cottage is today a kind of Coleridge shrine, would certainly have known about him. There was no time to explore the historic sites of Saint Omer; the next morning we moved on to Vottem, a suburb of Liége, in Belgium, where we were quartered in an empty police barracks. We stayed there for three weeks, preparing for our entry into Germany.

It was impressed on us very seriously that once we had crossed the German frontier we should be in danger of attack from Werewolves, the resistance fighters whom Himmler was supposed to be organizing. Should this happen, we must abandon our vehicles, taking with us only our Sten guns and ammunition, and seek cover in the nearest ditch. Early on the morning of Easter Sunday we moved off in convoy. In the middle of our convoy was a detachment of the RAF Regiment, each of their vehicles carrying a mounted Bren gun. The RAF Regiment were tough, professional fighting soldiers, many of them ex-Army men. Their job was to defend us amateur soldiers in any attack. It seemed to be understood, and rightly so, that our ability to defend ourselves did not amount to much. Fortunately, our capacity for doing so was not put to the test. Himmler's Werewolves were in fact a fiction; they never existed.

Our Intelligence Officer, Squadron-Leader Barber, accompanied by myself as supposed expert map-reader, had been designated to lead the convoy, but the CO, Group-Captain Howes, insisted on leading the way in his own jeep. We soon got lost, after we had crossed the German frontier, and nearly plunged over a bridge that had been cut in half by RAF bombing. We did not reach our destination until after dark, several hours late. It was lucky for us that no Werewolves had shown up. Our destination was the little town of Niedermendig, in the Eifel, where our officers were assigned to requisitioned billets and the rest of us were packed into the former Brown House, the local NSDAP (National Socialist Workers' Party) headquarters.

There was quite a comedy the next morning, when we were paraded for inspection by the CO. Someone shouted out that none of us had any soap. The Group-Captain turned to the Adjutant, Flight-Lieutenant Clough, and asked: "Mr Clough, why have the men no soap?" – "Soap, sir, soap?" replied the harrassed adjutant, who turned to the Station Warrant Officer and asked him: "Mr Brundell, why is there no soap?" – "Soap, sir, soap?", the SWO replied, and then put the same question to the Duty Flight-Sergeant, from whom it worked its way down to a humble corporal. Always the reply was the same: "Soap, sir, soap?" In the end the entire parade was so convulsed with laughter that it had to be dismissed by the CO, who saw the funny side of the matter himself. Later in the day a supply of soap was conjured up from somewhere. Requisitioned, no doubt.

We stayed only a week or two at Niedermendig, and then moved on to the Benedictine abbey of Maria Laach, not far from Koblenz. Romantically situated on the shores of the Laachersee, below wooded hills, the abbey had been founded in the year 1093. The fine Romanesque church, with five towers and a dome, was completed in 1156. In 1945 the community was still in residence, the war notwithstanding, though much reduced in numbers because many of the monks had been drafted into the German armed forces. In fact, it was about half its normal size, with about twenty choir-monks only, and fifty laybrothers. The full monastic liturgy was still being carried out, with daily sung mass and sung vespers, and high mass on Sundays.

The plainsong at Maria Laach is incomparably the best I have ever heard. The French monks of Solesmes are generally considered the finest exponents of Gregorian chant, but I have never thought them so myself; there is something too precious, too refined about their rendering, beautiful though it is. Of course, the German monks were using the Solesmes liturgical books, as the only ones that are officially approved by the Holy See; but how different was their interpretation. But then, the Germans disregarded the cardinal Solesmes principle that plainsong should be sung unaccompanied. At Maria Laach there was a discreet organ accompaniment, and what a difference it made.

The RAF occupied a wing of the monastery that had previously been occupied by the Wehrmacht. Painted on the roof was a large red cross, which we sensibly suffered to remain. Perhaps part of the building had been used previously as a German army hospital. But we did not stay long at Maria Laach; quite soon we moved on to the ancient small town of Wülfrath, twenty or so miles north of Düsseldorf. Here our Intelligence Section – four officers and four airmen – took over a very large office in a commercial building in the centre of the town. Other sections also had offices in the building, and the officers' mess was located on the ground floor. At first the CO, Group-Captain 'Charlie' Howes, was insistent that there must be no fraternizing with the civilian population; anyone caught talking to Germans would be severely dealt with, he assured us. This ban was widely breached from the start, but surreptitiously. The Rhinelanders are a friendly people, and we never experienced any hostility from them. Conversely, I never came across any airmen who felt hostile to the Germans. Nor was there among us any hatred of Hitler and the other German leaders. In fact, the people who were really unpopular with the British forces in Germany were Winston Churchill and Field Marshal Montgomery. Soldiers usually have a certain fellow-feeling and respect for their opposite numbers, the 'enemy'. In Wülfrath the 'no-fraternization' order collapsed once and for all on an evening when the CO was observed handing a mug of beer through the window of the officers' mess to the German policeman on duty outside.

We had no chaplains in our unit. On our first Sunday in Wülfrath it was given out that any airmen proposing to go to church must take with them, and keep with them all the time, their Sten guns and ammunition. Half a dozen or so of us made our way to the

Catholic church, a fair-sized modern building, with our Sten guns slung over our shoulders; but when we got to the church we could not bring ourselves to take these weapons with us into the house of God, so we left them piled up in the porch. Militarily, this was a very grave offence, liable to most severe punishment. If any of the weapons had been stolen we would have been in the direst trouble. However, when we left the church our weapons were all still there in the porch; and so it was on every Sunday afterwards.

Many of us soon had friends in the town who invited us to their houses of an evening. This was to our mutual advantage; for now it was the Germans, not ourselves, who lacked for soap, and tobacco also. We were now receiving ample rations of cigarettes – two hundred per man every fortnight – and plenty of soap, and these we used to exchange for bottles of Rhineland wine. Strong friendships were built up in this way.

We were not a large unit, and there was a good spirit of *camaraderie* among us. My colleagues in the Intelligence section, both officers and men, were easy to get on with. One of the SD clerks, William Warden, with whom I shared a room in a requisitioned house, was a professional water-colour painter, and he made many fine pictures of Rhineland scenes. I remember in particular one of Cologne Cathedral. In later years I used sometimes to wonder what had become of Bill Warden. In March 1985, when I was visiting a sick friend in Rye, I noticed in a shop window a poster advertising an exhibition of paintings by William Warden in one of the town's art galleries. I went to the gallery to make inquiries, and was told that Warden, who had been living near Rye, had died two years previously.

Before we left England I had decided that it would be sensible while in Germany to learn the language of the country, or something of it, and I had brought with me one or two elementary German textbooks. When we got to Wülfrath the weather was already quite warm; on my free afternoons I used to do my German study sitting on a bench in the Stadtpark. In this little park I made friends with two boys, one of whom, Willi Münch, who was thirteen, proved to be a good teacher of conversational German, and I learned much from him. After the war we kept in touch, and in 1950 he came to England and stayed with friends of mine in the Hertfordshire town of Ware. This led, when my friend and former pupil at Osmington School, Tring, Leo Kerrell-Vaughan, was mayor of Ware, to the 'twinning' of Ware and Wülfrath. In 1987 I was invited to attend the annual reunion of the two towns, when the burgomaster of Wülfrath and his councillors, and other citizens, were the guests of the Mayor and corporation, and people, of Ware. On this occasion I was able to renew my acquaintance and friendship with Herr Münch, now curator of the Wülfrath Folk Museum, well known also for his several published volumes of cartoons. In 1988, by kindness of Leo Kerrell-Vaughan, I was able to revisit Wülfrath in his company. The little town was much changed, much improved from its drab wartime condition, and was now very bright and full of life.

A bomb or two had fallen during the later stages of the war, but the ancient parish church, in Lutheran hands, had escaped damage. It had a fine organ, and one of my RAF friends, Harold Dawe, had spent many happy hours playing on it. Dawe was a Cornishman, from Chapel, near Launceston, and had a pleasing Cornish accent. After the war he signed on in the RAF, and rose to the rank of Warrant Officer. I never saw him again, but we kept in touch until his death. The Catholic church in Wülfrath was more or less bombed to the ground in the later stages of the war, and had been replaced by a big, and architecturally imposing, new structure.

At the beginning of this return to Wülfrath the new *pfarrer*, Pastor Schroeder, who came from Danzig, and had lived for thirteen years in Rome, and was a specialist in the history of art, received me very kindly, and invited me to concelebrate with him at the 10 o'clock sung Mass on Sunday morning. Fortunately, I was required to read only a very short part of the service; which was as well, for my knowledge of the German language had long since evaporated. However, it seems that I acquitted myself satisfactorily, for afterwards Pastor Schroeder told me that the next time I came he would ask me to preach. The German people's massbook seemed to me greatly superior to anything we had in England. In particular, the German canon of the mass is a much more dignified, not to say accurate, version of the Latin than is our own; and the many German hymns in the book, with their musical notation, seem to me to be of an altogether higher standard than most of the contents of our new English hymn-books.

While we were in Wülfrath we visited the Marian pilgrimage shrine at Neviges, a few kilometres distant. I had been there during the war, and was looking forward to seeing it again. The Neviges pilgrimage is centred on a much venerated and supposedly miraculous picture of the Blessed Virgin, which had been brought to Neviges in 1681. Formerly, as I remembered it, preserved in the baroque parish church adjoining the Franciscan friary, it has now been transferred to the new pilgrimage church, built in the 1960s. This huge, and exteriorly bizarre concrete structure, somewhat in the 'Gropius' style of architecture, can hold seven thousand people. There are no pillars supporting the roof, so everyone has a clear view of the sanctuary and high altar.

On this first, wartime visit to Neviges I had been accompanied by Harold Dawe and a *confrère* of ours, Bill Lingham. Willi Münch had kindly agreed to be our guide, as we had to walk, and were not sure of the way, which lay across country. On our way back, when dusk was setting in, a curious incident occurred. To appreciate it one must understand that the uniforms of the RAF and the Luftwaffe were of a rather similar shade of light blue, not easy to distinguish one from the other except in clear light. As we were walking along, happily engaged in conversation, a little, elderly German civilian stepped out from the bushes on one side of the road, and said excitedly: "*Marsch, haut ab, die Engländer sind immerschiert.*" (Clear off. You'd better scarper. We've been occupied by the English.)

The man who gave us this friendly warning was a certain Gustav Vogel, who had taken us for German Flaksoldaten (anti-aircraft gunners), whose uniform was similar to the Luftwaffe's. Gustav Vogel, who is now dead, was the man who used to repaint the old wooden farmhouses around Wülfrath every two years.

Before we left England we had been told that our unit was going to be attached to troops commanded by the American general George Patton. Patton was a 'controversial' personality, to put it mildly, and the prospect of being under his command was not reassuring. But by the time we got to Germany things had moved so fast that Patton and his army were, or were thought to be, in Bavaria. At any rate, we never saw them. At Wülfrath the town and countryside proved to be totally peaceful, and free from clandestine hostile activities; so there was not much for us to do. After a few months we moved north to Krefeld-Bochum, in the Ruhr, a very dreary industrial area where secret arms factories simply did not exist. Seeing that the war, at least in Europe, would soon end I began to think about what I should do when it was time to return to civilian life. One possibility was not to return to civilian life, but to sign on in the RAF for another twelve years, at the end of which time one would be able to retire with a pension. However, twelve years seemed to me to be a very long stretch of time, and I did not really feel that I was cut out to be a 'regular' airman. I had not lost my attraction to the religious life and the priesthood, and felt that I might now stand a better chance of success if I were to try again. However, mindful of Hilary Pepler's injunction, 'Never look back', I decided not to apply again to the Dominicans. Instead, I applied to the Canons Regular of the Lateran, and my application was accepted. The Prior of Bodmin applied to the Air Ministry for my early release, and I was demobilized in October 1945.

CHAPTER SEVEN

With the Austin Canons

IN November 1945, at the age of thirty-three, I entered the novitiate of the Canons Regular at the Priory of Saint Mary and Saint Petroc, Bodmin. There had been a priory of Austin Canons at Bodmin in the Middle Ages; nothing remains of it today except one or two broken pillars and a few stones in the park opposite the parish church. In 1881 the then Bishop of Plymouth entrusted the poor and struggling Roman Catholic mission of Bodmin to Dom Felix Menchini, a canon regular of the Lateran Congregation who had been exiled from Italy by anti-clerical laws. Menchini had arrived in England on his way, as he thought, to the United States; the bishop persuaded him to remain. He quickly recruited for his Order a young secular priest, Gilbert Higgins, who was chaplain to the Augustinian canonesses at Newton Abbot. With the aid of Fr Higgins, Menchini established a small community on land at the junction of two roads leading out of Bodmin town at its west end, and put up a temporary church, no very solid structure, that was supposed to last only until the means had been found to build something better. In the event, it was eighty years before it was replaced, and it still stands, serving now as the parish hall.

In 1900 things were going so badly with the Bodmin mission that there was talk of closing it down. It was saved by the efforts of Prior (later Abbot) Walter Aloysius Smith, who was in charge from 1900 to 1911, and built the larger portion of the adjacent canonry, which is a solid, handsome stone building of faintly castellated appearance. On the ground floor there is a spacious refectory, with windows looking into the garden, and a dignified common-room for the fathers, with a granite fireplace over which are carved the words *Cor unum et anima una in Deo*, from the Rule of Saint

Augustine, which quotes them from The Acts of the Apostles. From the ground floor a small cloister led into the old church, which was superseded by the new one in the 1960s.

The first floor of the priory was given over to the cells of the professed priests and laybrothers. In 1945 there was only one brother. The Prior's cell was spacious, with his sleeping quarters curtained off. It was the custom when entering the prior's cell to genuflect to him before speaking. Also on the first floor was an oratory, or small chapel, which was used for private Masses, and for the community's morning and evening meditation, and night prayers. It had a barrelled roof, and a rather fine Gothic west window. Facing the oratory was the library, an addition to the original building, the creation of Dom Richard Alphonsus McElroy, the 'great' prior of Bodmin. As a room the library was not very large, but it housed a fine collection of books, with a good range of works on Cornish history, topography, archaeology, flora and fauna, and so on. One must sorrowfully record that since *le néfaste concile* things at Bodmin, as with so many other religious houses, have somewhat fallen off. The numbers of the community are very much reduced, and the priory's six or seven parishes dependent have been surrendered to the diocese.

Father McElroy had entered the Order after some years in business in Liverpool. He was a tall, handsome man, of considerable cultivation, an excellent administrator and man of affairs. As well as being prior, he was also the rural dean of the area, and was well known and greatly respected throughout Cornwall. He had written the first biography of Cuthbert Mayne. In the late 1930s he organized a summer school of Celtic religious studies in Truro, with lectures by Abbot Anscar Vonier, of Buckfast, Dom Louis Gougaud, of Farnborough Abbey, Archbishop Alban Goodier, SJ, and other scholars. Nothing of this kind had been attempted by Catholics in Cornwall before. In 1937 Fr McElroy had begun the building of a new priory church at Bodmin, and had carried out on behalf of the Abbot General of the Canons Regular of the Lateran a visitation of canonical houses in South America. This task he had accomplished so well that it was understood that he would be created Abbot at the next General Chapter of the Order. At that point he went into Saint Michael's Hospital, at Hayle, for a prostate operation. Apart from this, he appeared to be in excellent health. During the first night that he was away a large framed print of Saint Monica that hung in his room fell down, and its glass covering was smashed. When this was discovered the next morning one or two members of the community felt a certain unease; so they were not altogether surprised when later in the day the news was received that the Prior had died without recovering from the operation. Lacking the superintending presence of Dom McElroy the building of the new church soon ran into difficulties. The builder went bankrupt, and when the war came the whole project was suspended for the duration, and well beyond. Eventually, work on the church was begun again, and in due time completed. But the building's design had been much modified; the result was not the church of Fr McElroy's dreams.

The top floor of the priory was given over to the novitiate. The cells were quite as austere as those at Woodchester; the novice master had only one room, but it was larger than the others. From the windows of the cells you could see in the distance the conical white china-clay mounds outside St Austell. The novitiate common room filled the length of the building from south to north, and was big enough to have space for a table-tennis table. The novitiate library was more amply stocked than that at Woodchester, but its contents, as was to be expected, were more edifying than exciting. It contained few recent publications.

The pattern of life in noviciates was much the same everywhere; perhaps it still is, but the pattern has changed. Except in the monasteries of monks there seems to be very little left now of the old claustral discipline. In 1945 the novice master at Bodmin was Dom William Rowe, a Yorkshireman of proven merit. He was something of a musician, and had previously been headmaster of Saint Augustine's School, at Datchet, near Windsor. He was an understanding and witty man, who exacted a proper standard of discipline from his charges, but without severity. The prior, Dom Charles White, was a youngish London-Irishman. He was a keen bee-keeper, and looked after the priory's thirty hives. He was a good cricketer too, and played for Bodmin Town. He had a fine singing voice. A high point in Holy Week at Bodmin was always Prior White's singing of the 'Oratio Jeremiae Prophetae' in the office of Tenebrae for Holy Saturday. This he always sang to the more elaborate solemn *ad libitum* tone.

The oldest member of the community, Dom George McGregor, was a native of Bodmin, and a Roman doctor of divinity. There were usually five or six priests in residence, and a similar, or slightly smaller number of postulants and novices. In 1945 there was also a laybrother, Brother Patrick Tully-Ellis, and a lay *familiaris*, Mr Bye. There were also seven non-resident canons who lived out, in their parishes, which were dependent on the priory: Launceston, St Ives, St Austell, Bude, Newquay, and Swanage, this last being in Dorset. The non-resident canons returned to the priory for the annual eight days' retreat, and once a month for a day of recollection, and a meeting of the chapter.

Christmas was always well kept up at the priory, for the whole Twelve Days. Noviciate rules were relaxed, and the novices were allowed the freedom of the fathers' common-room. They were allowed to smoke – something normally prohibited, and a serious offence – and on Christmas Day and Saint Stephen's Day, if I remember correctly, drinks were dispensed: with due moderation.

A principal feature of the Christmas festivities was the game of 'Obadiah'. In this game two players lie on their sides, on the floor, blindfolded and facing each other, with their left hands joined. In his right hand each holds a long, stiff wand, made of tightly rolled-up newspaper. When both are in position and ready, the first player shouts: "Are you there, Obadiah?", to which the other responds "Yes", while at the same time he rolls over, but without disjoining his left hand, so as to avoid a hearty thwack from the other man's wand. The first to be struck leaves the game, and is replaced by another. This game, which the spectators always find very diverting, has only one drawback: at the end, the floor is covered with fragments of newspaper, which it takes some time to clear up afterwards.

Another major annual event was the feast of Saint Agnes, the fourth century virgin-martyr whose relics are preserved in the Roman basilica of Sant' Agnese *fuore i muri*, which is served by the Lateran Canons. On this day, 21st January, custom required that the novices should invite the fathers, and other professed members of the community, to tea in the novitiate common-room. A meal of some elegance and substance was expected. Its preparation required much thought and effort. It was *de rigueur* that after the meal the novices should entertain their seniors; it might be with charades, a concert, some enacted scenes from Shakespeare, or even an original one-act play. Of course, in a year when there were only two or three novices the proceedings had to be simplified. In my year we substituted a magic-lantern show with views of famous churches and shrines. In an attempt, which was successful, to make the audience laugh, a view of Manchester Cathedral was shown at repeated intervals.

An essential element in the life of canons regular is the solemn celebration of the liturgy. At Bodmin one was very carefully trained in such matters. On days of high festival, such as the feast of Saint Petroc on 14th July, or that of Saint Augustine of Hippo on 28th August, things were really done very well indeed, with the assistance of the non-resident canons, who attended the High Mass on such days, and the celebratory luncheon that followed. At the mass the singing of the hymn 'Magne Pater Augustine' used to be quite thunderous. It went to a very joyful tune, which seemed to be peculiar to the Order's English province. The tune to which it was sung on the Continent was quite melancholy by contrast.

On Sundays, however, the celebration of the liturgy was not as solemn as might have been wished because some of the priests had to leave the house to serve various dependent chapels or small churches where there was no resident priest, as at Padstow, Par, Wadebridge, Fowey, and Tintagel. Some of them had to celebrate two masses, each in a different place. For middle-aged, and sometimes elderly men, not always in the best of health, this could be exacting, for in those days the celebrant at mass had to be fasting from the previous midnight. It was a great concession, and a great blessing, when the Holy See gave permission for a drink of tea or coffee to be taken between the services.

At home on Sunday morning there would often be only two priests available, one to celebrate the 8 o'clock Low Mass, the other the 11 o'clock Sung Mass. The priest who had celebrated and preached at the early mass had to take charge of and sustain the rather uncertain little choir of novices at the later service. This task usually fell to Father John Daly, a young Scots canon with a good voice whose poor health precluded him from serving any of the external missions. For some time we were puzzled by his habit of leaving the sanctuary after the Gospel, and returning only after the sermon. It took us a little while to discover that during this interval he went out into the fresh air for a smoke. On high festivals there was always Sung Vespers; and the normal Sunday evening service was Sung Compline, followed by sermon and Benediction.

An honoured guest at the high table in the refectory on major festal occasions was Mr Arthur Tremayne, an aged and impoverished Cornish gentleman with silver hair and beard. It was said of him that he should have inherited considerable wealth, but had been disinherited on account of his conversion to the Catholic faith. We were always glad to see this quiet, friendly old man, who was held in special regard by the community. Once a year he came to stay at the priory for a week, to make his annual retreat. He was always up early in the morning. In the church he followed all the offices, reading in his missal and breviary with the help of a magnifying glass. He was courteous and affable to all. In Mr Tremayne we recognized a holy confessor of the faith.

For a good part of my novitiate year there was only one other novice, Roy Dunstan, a man of about my own age who had served in the Merchant Navy during the war. Eventually we were joined by three or four others. At the beginning of our novitiate Dunstan and myself had been invested by the Prior with the white cassock and linen rochet which are the distinctive garb of the Canons Regular of the Lateran. The white cassock was worn on Sundays and solemnities only; on ordinary days a black cassock was worn. But on Sundays and major feasts the rochet – a sort of narrow-sleeved surplice – and the white cassock were worn even in the refectory. Birettas also were worn in the refectory, as well as in choir.

In the refectory there was the customary reading at meals; but on Sundays, holy days, and other more or less special occasions, the Prior could allow conversation. The reading was not done from a raised pulpit, as at Woodchester, but from a reading-desk in the middle of the refectory. This reading-desk was low enough to allow of the reader's sitting down, on a wooden stool. As at Woodchester, on Fridays the Rule of Saint Augustine was read in its entirety at the mid-day meal. There was just time to get through it if your Latin was proficient; otherwise it had to be finished at supper. (Once a month it was read in English for the benefit of the lay-brothers.)

On Saturdays an extract, of whose length the Prior was judge, was read from the sonorous-sounding *Constitutiones Canonicorum*

Regularium Ordinis Sancti Augustini Congregationis Sanctissimi Salvatoris Lateranensis. Saint Augustine's Rule laid great emphasis on charity as the norm and end of community life – '*Ante omnia, fratres carissimi, diligatur Deus, deinde et proximus*' – and on the exact observance of the common life, with strict avoidance of private ownership. The Constitutions legislated in more detail for the canonical life, and even dealt with such minutiae as behaviour at meals: for instance, it was forbidden to speak across your neighbour at table to the man on his other side. It was also forbidden to leave the canonry on days of public holiday; but this injunction probably had more in mind Naples during *Carnivale* than Bodmin on a Bank Holiday. I do not think it was taken too seriously. A purely local rule, peculiar to the Priory of Saint Mary and Saint Petroc, inhibited members of the community from going to the cinema in Bodmin town. Breach of this regulation brought down on the delinquent an excommunication, release from which was reserved to the Prior. I never heard of anyone incurring this censure.

In April 1947 Dom Roy Dunstan and myself were admitted to temporary vows, binding us to the Order for the next three years only. A week later we left Bodmin for the Order's house of studies at Hoddesdon, in Hertfordshire. Saint Augustine's Priory, formerly named Esdale House, was an ugly Victorian yellow-brick mansion in the little town's main street. Next door, in Rawdon House, built in the Restoration era by one Sir Marmaduke Rawdon, and now renamed Saint Monica's Priory, was a community of Canonesses of the Lateran-Windesheim Congregation, which had links with the Venerable Thomas â Kempis, author of the *Imitatio Christi.* Sadly, this historic community was dissolved, for lack of sufficient numbers, some years ago, and Rawdon House is now an old people's home.

Esdale House had been acquired by Abbot Smith in 1930 as a house of studies for the Order. In 1947 the normal two years' course of scholastic philosophy was taught there, after which the student-canons went on to Saint Edmund's College, near Ware, for their theology. The canons regular were in charge of the Roman Catholic parish at Hoddesdon, but as yet there was no church. On weekdays Mass and the divine office were celebrated in the priory's domestic chapel, which was open to the public. On Sundays Mass and Benediction were held in the parish primary school at the bottom of the garden.

The large garden was the most attractive feature of the Esdale House property. There was a big lawn and a tennis court, and on its west side the garden was lined by fine trees. The house itself, a most unprepossessing building, was built on the 'well' principle; that is, from the big hall on the ground floor one looked straight up to the skylight in the roof. Each floor consisted of a landing built around the central 'well', with rooms radiating off. Legend had it that in earlier days someone had committed suicide by jumping off the top landing. One could readily believe it; the 'atmosphere' of the house was most depressing.

The first superior at Saint Augustine's, in 1930, had been an exiled Dutch or German canon regular, Dom Bruno Peters, who had previously been a Premonstratensian canon regular. Dom Bruno was a man of iron, a stringent disciplinarian. There were many stories about him, none of them likely to reassure anyone who was about to come under his care. For example, he would send the students out on their monthly all-day walk in the Hertfordshire countryside with only sixpence each for the purchase of food and drink. When he accompanied them himself, as he sometimes did, he was not above ordering glasses of water in a café, thinking tea too expensive. Certainly he himself *coude in litel thing han suffisaunce.'*

Father Bruno's command of the English language was imperfect; he once managed in the course of a sermon to convert the phrase 'by fits and starts' into a spoonerism which considerably astonished the congregation. By 1947, though, he had retired to Christchurch Priory, Eltham; on his occasional visits to Hoddesdon we found him a benign old gentleman who loved to tell us of the pioneer days of the Order's restoration in England. Time had mellowed him.

Another notable previous superior had been Dom Vincent Scully DSO, a former army chaplain of the first war. Father Scully had a great devotion to the Venerable Thomas â Kempis, some of whose works he had translated into English. An energetic man, and a zealous parish priest, he upheld the Order's contemplative tradition and ancient customs. He was perhaps the last of the canons in England to wear white stockings with the white cassock. He was sometimes criticized for the length of his sermons, but in all other respects he was a pattern canon regular.

In the spring of 1947 there was a kind of interregnum at Saint Augustine's Priory. Father Peters had left, Father Scully also, and had been succeeded by Fr McGregor, from Bodmin, whose years – he was now over seventy – were beginning to tell on him. Fr McGregor's was a temporary appointment; but when his successor, a much younger man, arrived he continued in residence as regent of studies. He was a big, white-haired man of considerable dignity and presence. In spite of, or perhaps partly because of, certain foibles he was a lovable personality. Many years earlier it had seemed likely that he would be made Abbot; and he never really got over his chagrin when the mitre was bestowed instead on 'that man Smith', which was his usual way of referring to his right reverend *confrère* the titular Abbot of Saint Mary *in pratis*, Leicester, the house in which Cardinal Wolsey had taken refuge and died. Fr McGregor must have been supremely confident of the appointment, since in preparation for it he had provided himself with a pectoral cross and chain, and an abbatial ring. These items he kept in a drawer in his room until the end of his life. In choir, and in the refectory, on Sundays and festal days, he always wore a rochet with a deep fringe of lace, and buckled shoes, the special prerogative of abbots. It says much for Fr McGregor's simplicity and goodness that people were not offended, but mildly amused by these pretentions. George McGregor was a very kind and charitable man; and it is charity rather than strict adherence to canon law and constitutions that makes the good religious. Fr McGregor was notable also for his strong, deep, melodious singing voice. I remember him officiating at Benediction in the Canonesses' chapel at Hoddesdon, where our students used to act as altar servers on occasion, when he would provide an elaborate and powerful descant to the hymn 'Tantum ergo', sung amid clouds of incense to Haydn's 'Deutschland über alles' melody.

After we had been at Hoddesdon a few weeks the new superior arrived. A week or so later a parishioner rather tactlessly asked Fr McGregor: "How do you like being second-in-command now?" To which he good-humouredly replied: "Oh, that's all right. *He* sits in the chair; *I* make the decisions." His successor was no doubt tactful in allowing him to think so.

We now began our course in the various branches of scholastic philosophy: logic, cosmology, epistemology, ethics, and psychology, which were taught *ad mentem divi Thomae*, in conformity with the mind of Saint Thomas Aquinas. We had an excellent teacher in Dom Anthony Smith, a young canon who held a Roman licentiate in divinity. He was assisted by a young Brazilian canon, Dom Garmendia, who later became an auxiliary bishop in the diocese of New York. These two laid well the philosophical groundwork for the course of theology that we were to follow at Saint Edmund's College.

Our new superior was with us for a short time only; he was soon transferred back to Cornwall to fill another post. There was much speculation among the students – for there were five or six of us now – as to who would succeed him. When the next prior's name was announced we were a good deal surprised, for the man in question, a member of the Bodmin community, was considered to be something of an invalid. Nor had he ever been superior of a community before. He certainly learned the craft of superiorship the hard way, and his term of office at Hoddesdon was not altogether a success; but he was a man of character and ability, not easily discouraged; eventually he rose to high office in the Order.

At Hoddesdon, though, the odds were against him, for he was expected to combine in himself the offices of prior, parish priest, bursar, and master of the students: a near-impossible assignment, one would have thought. There were now seven students in all: four older men – what would now be called 'mature students' – a young man of twenty-two, and two teenagers straight from Saint Augustine's School at Datchet. Of the older men two, Dom Roy Dunstan and Dom Herbert Seaton, had served in the Merchant Navy during the war. Dom Edward Kelly, a native of Ireland, had not been quite old enough for wartime military service, but had worked for some years in the construction industry. To manage a group of such diverse ages would have been difficult for any superior; so it was hardly surprising that our new and inexperienced prior never quite found the way. His method was to treat us all alike, more or less as if we were all teenagers. This created difficulties both for us and for him.

In our student group there was one man of exceptional intellectual calibre, Dom Victor Main, who was twenty-two at this time. He was sometimes known by his Christian name, Douglas; but he had assumed his religious name, Victor, as a gesture of pious respect to the medieval mystical writers of the Victorine school: Hugh of Saint Victor, Richard of Saint Victor, Adam and Walter of Saint Victor, all of them canons of the abbey of Saint Victor in Paris. Douglas had been born in London, of Irish parents, in 1926. He was a very tall, erect young man, and wore rimless spectacles. He had been educated at the Westminster Cathedral Choir School, to which he had won a choral scholarship, and then by the Jesuits at Saint Ignatius's College, Stamford Hill. Musically he was very accomplished, so he was a great help to our small plainsong choir.

On leaving school he went into journalism, and got a job on his local paper, the *Hornsey Journal*. In the course of his work he got to know Abbot Smith and the other canons regular at Stroud Green. In 1943 he enlisted in the Royal Corps of Signals; after the war he felt a call to the priesthood, and joined the canons regular at Bodmin. He was a brilliant student, and a very agreeable *confrère* to live with. He never seemed to be out of humour; if he ever was, he did not show it. There was a certain reserve about him, and he never had much to say about his quite large family, or his experiences as a reporter for the *Hornsey Journal*; but just occasionally he would give us a tiny glimpse of his past life. One story that he used occasionally to tell always amused me, and as it does not appear in his biography, *In the Stillness Dancing* by Neil McKenty, I will give it here.

Before his *Hornsey Journal* days Douglas had been employed for a time at Dunn and Company's big hat shop in the Strand. The manager, who wore a stiff winged collar and had a waxed moustache with upturned ends, was a martinet, and kept his underlings subject to a strict discipline. The task the employees most dreaded was having to dress the shop's great front window, facing onto the pavement thronged with passers-by, many of whom would stop to watch what was going on. This window-dressing was an important element in the training of Dunn and Company's young men. It could take several hours, for nothing less than absolute perfection was required. It was not unlike a class in Constance Spry flower-arrangement; any clumsiness in the positioning of the hats, or their awkward grouping on the various pegs and stands inside the window, would drive the manager to frenzied imprecation and gesticulation, all much enjoyed by the fascinated idlers on the pavement outside.

On one particular window-dressing day things had gone particularly badly, leaving the shop-assistants worn out and dispirited. But eventually the manager bade them stop, telling Douglas to come outside with him onto the pavement. There the manager stood with folded arms, Douglas beside him, in rapt contemplation of the new window-display. For a minute or so they stood there in silence, and then Douglas heard the manager say, in reverent tones: "There they are. Just like a flock of birds!"

From Hoddesdon Douglas was sent to Rome for his theological studies; but there something went wrong, and he left the Order. It is not clear why. One heard it said that he had some difficulty over the interpretation of the vow of common life, the equivalent of the vow of poverty in other orders; but others blamed it on a mild practical joke that he played on a rather pompous prior of Bodmin who was visiting Rome.

After resuming the secular state Douglas Main read law at Trinity College, Dublin; later, at the Inns of Court in London, he qualified as a barrister. In 1954 he joined the British Colonial Service. While in Malaya he discovered the mystical tradition of Eastern religion, which affected him profoundly. On his return from Malaya he became a Benedictine monk at Ealing Abbey, in West London. While there he was asked to become headmaster of Saint Anselm's Abbey School at Washington, D.C., a monastery of the English Benedictine Congregation. After he had been there some years a Canadian bishop invited him to Montreal, where he founded a monastery on a more 'open' pattern than usual, and started a school for spirituality which attracted a wide following. His death, from cancer, at the age of fifty-six was a great loss to religion. His influence lives on.

A younger *confrère* who was much liked at Hoddesdon was Dom Robert Hawkes, who joined the Order from the school at Datchet. He was in every way a most promising religious; but he left, after being dispensed from his temporary vows, because of scruples over the vow of celibacy. He was so good-looking that probably this was very sensible; but, sadly, he died of nephritis at the age of twenty-nine. He had been told many years before that it was not likely that he would live to be forty. From that point of view it was a pity that he left the Order, which gave him the kind of quiet, secure routine that he needed. While at Saint Augustine's, Hoddesdon, he

especially distinguished himself by the care he gave to nursing
Father McGregor during his last illness: no easy task.

Dom Edward Kelly, who had reached Hoddesdon earlier than
the rest of us, was an acute Irishman, by temperament, I would
think, not unlike Oliver Goldsmith, on whose life and work he
was, and is, a considerable authority. He was the best classical
scholar among us, a fact that he mostly contrived to keep to
himself. He and I had a rather similar sense of humour; at feast day
meals we would sometimes keep our fellow-students amused by our
banter, which was not at all appreciated by our superior. Which
was odd, as he was much given to wisecracks and witticisms
himself.

At Saint Augustine's Priory the life was arduous and the studies
exacting. We rose at 5.30 a.m. In addition to the philosophy course
I was also doing a correspondence course of study for the London
University matriculation exam. The manual labour that we did on
most afternoons was no formality either. None of us liked gardening
much; but it was made bearable by the opportunities it gave us of
talking with our Cockney gardener, Mr Aldridge, who had been one
of the original 'Old Contemptibles' of the 1914-18 war. He liked
to show us the letters he received from time to time from the
Old Contemptibles Association. (The Kaiser was supposed to have
referred in 1914 to the British Expeditionary Force as 'a contemptible little army', but this is now known to have been a piece of
British government anti-German propaganda.) These letters were
addressed to him as 'Chum Aldridge', such being their convention.
He had a fund of reminiscence and anecdote, which somehow
seemed not to stale with repetition; and he loved to tell us of how
he had been appointed the Colonel's runner, since he was the
fastest man in the regiment.

Unhappily, a day came when Chum Aldridge was summarily
dismissed from our employment. His downfall was brought about
by Dom Philip Corr, an aged canon who had come to settle among
us after thirty years as parish priest at Swanage. He was a fanatic-
ally keen gardener. At Hoddesdon gardening was his chosen occupation from dawn to dusk, except in bad weather. He was puzzled
and distressed by the students' lack of interest in matters horti-
cultural, and had little sympathy with our occasional mildly-voiced
complaints about not having enough time for study. It was his boast

that he had not opened a book since he was ordained, which must have been at least fifty years previously. Certainly his only reading matter now appeared to be the *Daily Telegraph* and the *Homiletic Review*, an American publication from which he got his sermon material.

On gardening matters Fr Corr and Mr Aldridge by no means saw eye to eye, and the Old Contemptible was much tried by what he regarded as interference on the part of the venerable clerk in holy orders. One day things came to a head, and Chum Aldridge was provoked into replying in terms somewhat military to Fr Corr's criticism of his methods. And that was the end of his association with the Canons Regular. We greatly missed his cheerful company, which had enlivened for us many a dreary afternoon.

The two years' philosophy course passed quickly, and in September 1949 the six senior students began the four years' course of theology at Saint Edmund's College, Old Hall Green. We drove over to Saint Edmund's every morning from Monday to Friday, except for Thursday, which was set aside for private study. The first lecture was at nine o'clock, and we were back in Hoddesdon for lunch at one. There were no lectures in the afternoon. Saint Edmund's was one of the most historic of the English Catholic seminaries. (I say 'was' because the seminary was closed down after the second Vatican Council, for lack of students, and was later re-opened, on a much reduced scale, in an empty convent in Chelsea.) The college had been founded at Douai, in France, in 1568, to educate and train secular priests for the English mission. In 1793 the college had to be abandoned on account of the war between France and England; by then the penal laws against Catholics had been somewhat relaxed. The buildings at Old Hall Green date from 1795. The splendid neo-Gothic chapel, by Pugin, was built in 1845.

In the cloisters of the college are the tombs and monuments of the later Vicars Apostolic of the London District: bishops William Poynter, James Yorke Bramston, his coadjutor Robert Gradwell, and James Talbot. And those of former presidents of the college: among them James Laird Patterson, Bishop of Emmaeus, and Dr Fenton, Bishop of Amycla, who is mentioned in Lytton Strachey's essay on Cardinal Manning. In the Galilee chapel, an extension of Pugin's fane, is the tomb of Cardinal Bourne, who was especially

devoted to the welfare of Saint Edmund's. In the college one felt
that one was at the heart of native English Catholicism, and that
here, if anywhere, one would find its authentic spirit and tradition.
I do not know where one would find them today. We canons regular
were made very welcome by the President, Monsignor Bagshawe,
and the professors, and by 'the divines', as the divinity students
were called. We never had any feeling of being outsiders, or not
truly belonging.

The two principal lecturers in the divinity faculty were Canon
George Smith and Canon Edward Mahoney, who taught, respectively, dogmatic and moral theology. Canon Smith, a most lucid
lecturer, was reputed one of the most learned theologians in the
country. His lectures were never dull; but his personality rarely
obtruded. Canon Mahoney's lecture-hall manner was very different;
it was highly idiosyncratic, and he kept his hearers' attention by
means of a flow of apposite reminiscences, anecdotes, and jokes.
His handling of the difficult treatise *de matrimonio*, which dealt
with such matters as divorce, annulment of marriage, birth control,
and sexual deviations was both careful and candid.

In 1949 Dr Smith and Dr Mahoney were nearing the end of the
many years they had spent at Saint Edmund's; now they are both
dead. I count it a privilege to have been able to study under the
guidance of two such learned and able teachers, who were at the
same time exemplary priests. Canon Mahoney seemed rather to
take to Dom Edward Kelly and myself; I cannot think why, unless it
was that we were good students and happened to appreciate his
very individual sense of humour. From time to time we would be
invited to call on him on a Thursday afternoon at his cottage in the
grounds of a nearby convent-school where he was chaplain, to
listen to records of classical music from his large collection, and
enjoy a cup of tea. As far as I know, none of the resident divines at
Saint Edmund's was ever accorded this privilege.

Back in Hoddesdon we were now receiving lessons in Hebrew
from an Italian canon regular, Don Angelo Penna, a delightful
man who was just beginning to make for himself an international
reputation as a biblical scholar, a reputation that was to be consoli-
dated by his books on the Maccabees and on Saint Paul. It was six
months before I could make anything of the Hebrew language at
all; then, suddenly, something seemed to click in my mind, and I

began to get the hang of it. Just at that point Fr Penna was recalled to Rome, and that was the end of our Hebrew classes.

About this time the authorities at Saint Edmund's informed our superiors that if one of our number should again fail his examinations, he would not this time be allowed to re-sit them, and would not be admitted to the college for the next academic year. This man, for whom study was really difficult, had the makings of a good priest, and our superiors did not wish to lose him. Also at this time community life at Saint Augustine's had become rather unsettled; there was a good deal of tension in the house, and two or three students left. Those in charge decided to solve both these problems by the drastic expedient of sending us back to Bodmin, to complete our studies there.

Saint Mary's Priory was not a house of studies; but there were just enough priests there with some kind of academic qualification to equip it for this purpose. Actually, we had had at Saint Edmund's *two* students who had difficulty in acquiring the *scientia debita*; at Bodmin it would be possible for them to receive more individual attention. The solution seemed drastic; but it was for the best in the circumstances. And although most of us were deeply sorry at the prospect of having to leave Saint Edmund's, we were not sorry to leave Esdale House, otherwise known as Saint Augustine's Priory. Some years later the canons regular gave up the parish and left Hoddesdon. The diocese of Westminster then sold the house, which was eventually razed to the ground. We will take our leave of Esdale House with this letter, which appeared in *The Times* of 31 March 1975.

ETERNAL BRIGHTNESS

From the Reverend Edward Kelly

Sir, The letter from the Reverend Mr Beer (March 24th) concerning an electric light bulb which still continues to function, though of considerable longevity as such things go, reminds me of a much older bulb. When I was a student, in Hoddesdon, it was bought for a penny, in a jumble sale, during the autumn of 1930, and suspended from a corridor ceiling by a stout piece of flex. It was considered a feat to strike it with your biretta in passing, and something of an achievement to smack it smartly with the palm of the hand, setting it swaying like a clock pendulum. It rebounded gaily from ceiling and walls which, in the course of time, developed many indentations.

For over thirty years the bulb withstood the harassments of students, the cavalier incompetence of workmen with trestles and ladders, and the furious spring-cleaning vendettas of domestic staff. It survived the vicissitudes of the war, when bombs were falling all round, and the doors and windows often ceased to fulfill the purpose for which they were designed; the bulb still continued to cast its rays of scorn over these manifestations of the power of Hitler.

Eventually the college was closed and the students dispersed, but, as we left, the bulb was staring reproachfully after us, like an elderly gentleman putting on a brave show. When, later, the building was demolished, no amount of effort could separate the bulb from its socket, and, eventually, it disappeared among the demolition débris.

Somewhere among the rubble of our main motor-ways languishes the little bulb which gave more than thirty years of active service, and which, I firmly believe, would once more, with the aid of a very small electric impulse, cast a little light upon our very darkened world.

Yours etc.
EDWARD KELLY

St Peter-in-Chains
12 Womersley Road
Hornsey, N8

In January 1952 I was temporarily transferred from Bodmin to the abbey of Bouhay, the house of studies of the Franco-Belgian province of the Lateran Canons, at Bressoux, a suburb of Liége, in Belgium. There was some idea that after my ordination I might teach in the school at Datchet, so it was thought desirable that I should improve my knowledge of French. The abbey stands on a hill overlooking the main street of Bressoux, and is a large, imposing building. The church, which has a lofty tower, with a carillon of bells, is over a hundred years old; but the canonry is of more recent date, and was built from the proceeds of a lottery. It is a spacious and dignified edifice; but in the 1950s it had its draw-backs, notably in the matter of sanitation. In summer the water supply was apt to give out, so that for days on end it was not possible to flush the toilets. There was no running water in the rooms, and cold water only was available for washing in. And there was only one bathroom, if you could call it that: for it was a kind of cellar. The taking of baths was not among the abbey's traditions. Should you wish to take a bath you had to ask the cook, a secular employee, to light a special fire to heat the water; and this he was usually not very willing to do. In the heat of summer life became difficult.

In 1952 the community numbered ten priests, eight students, and three or four laybrothers. Most of its members were Dutch. Liége is in the Walloon part of Belgium, where the people tend, by and large, to be socialist and anti-clerical, and provide few recruits to the clergy or religious orders. The Canons Regular of the Lateran have no houses in Flanders, the strongly Catholic part of Belgium; but their house at Sluys, in Holland, is a source of Dutch vocations. However, the language of the house at Bouhay was French, and all sermons were preached in French. The reading in the refectory was in French, and I was assigned to this duty within a week of my arrival. My pronunciation seemed not too bad, but I profited greatly from fairly frequent correction.

When I arrived in Liége the abbacy of Bouhay was vacant. Its previous incumbent, the late Abbot Roy, had been a ruling abbot (abbot *de regimine*), not a titular abbot, and had combined in his own person the offices of Visitor (or Provincial) of the Franco-Belgian province CRL, Abbot of Bouhay, Bursar at Bouhay, Master of Students and Novices, and Prior of the independent Priory of Saint Catharine in the city of Liége. This pluralism had not been a happy experience for the abbey's community, so there was a certain delay in the appointment of a new abbot, the prior being left in control. But I had not been there long before a new abbot, a titular abbot this time, was blessed. (This meant that the house would remain under the jurisdiction of the prior, with the abbot presiding, in the church and in the refectory, as a kind of paterfamilias; by no means a bad arrangement.) I had not seen the rite for the blessing of an abbot before, and it is a very interesting one. The Bishop of Liége, Monseigneur Kerkhofs, officiated, with the assistance, as is required, of two other abbots, in this instance, one a Benedictine monk, the other a Premonstratensian canon regular. From then on we had the added splendour of pontifical rites in the church on the greater festivals.

After I had been in Belgium some months I became greatly attracted, not for the first time, by the spirit and traditions of the Carmelite Order. I had been reading the life of Saint John of the Cross by Père Bruno de Jésus-Marie, a Flemish discalced Carmelite, and I had been impressed by what I had seen and heard when I visited the Marian pilgrimage shrine run by the friars of the discalced Carmelite observance at Chèvremont, a few kilometres from Liége. And in the city of Liége one came across memories and legends of the great fifteenth century prior general of the Carmelite Order, Blessed John Soreth. Of all the cities of Europe in which his Order had been established, Liége had been his favourite.

I had first come across the Order in 1934, when I was at Ditchling. One summer day a large black car had drawn up outside Saint Dominic's Press, and from it there emerged two clergymen. I was standing in the composing room, near the door, when they knocked, and when I opened it the taller of the two announced, in a strong Irish accent: "I am Father Lynch of Faversham, so I am." He had come, he explained, to seek advice, because he was thinking of setting up in Faversham a printing office to take care of his Order's needs in that respect. Why he should have chosen to seek this advice from a small private press, where no modern machinery was in use, is not clear. Probably he had heard vaguely of Saint Dominic's Press as a 'Catholic' enterprise, where he could expect to be received sympathetically. Kentish printers might have regarded him as a potential rival and competitor. At any rate, he was able to confer with Hilary Pepler, and in due time his visit to Ditchling resulted in the setting up of the Carmelite Press in Faversham.

Before he left for home later that afternoon Father Lynch, who no doubt was on the lookout for recruits to his Order, invited me to visit him at Faversham. Not long afterwards I spent a few days there at Whitefriars, a fine old Georgian house, from *c.* 1735, to which Father Lynch had contrived, by means of skilful adaptations, to give quite a monastic appearance and atmosphere. It was not long before I wrote to ask him if I could be considered as a candidate for admission to the Carmelite Order. His reply was encouraging, but he had to refer the matter to his prior provincial in Dublin, and back the answer came: No English recruits required at the present time, thank you. So the matter got no further.

In 1951 the Carmelites in England had gained their independence from Ireland, and were able to set up their own novitiate at Aylesford Priory, in Kent. Learning of this I decided, after much reflection, to seek permission to transfer from the Canons Regular to the Carmelites. This required the assent of the Abbot General of the CRL and the Prior General of the Carmelites, and in addition a dispensation from the Holy See. All this took time to negotiate, but in December 1952 I was admitted to the Carmelite Order as a novice, at Aylesford, where I exchanged the cassock and rochet of the Canons Regular for the brown habit and white *cappa* of the Whitefriars, at the same time being assigned the monastic name of Brocard, after the saint who was prior of the hermits of Mount Carmel at the beginning of the thirteenth century.

Transfers from one religious order to another are not particularly unusual. For some people, finding their proper niche in the religious life takes time, and involves a process of trial and error. To the Canons Regular I owe much: not least a first-rate ecclesiastical education.

CHAPTER EIGHT

A Roman Interlude

In November 1949 the medieval Carmelite friary at Aylesford, a village in Kent, six miles east of the cathedral city of Rochester, was recovered by the Order after it had been for four centuries in a succession of private hands. A large part of the monastery had disappeared during the private occupation, and the church had been demolished by the first secular owner; but a substantial part of the old buildings remained.

The recovery of the friary for the Order was due to the initiative of Fr Elias Lynch, the oldest and most remarkable of three remarkable brothers, from County Wicklow in Ireland, who all rose to prominent positions in the Order. In 1926 a few Irish friars had come to Kent to take charge of the Roman Catholic parishes in Faversham and Sittingbourne, which are not far from Aylesford, where the former priory was of special interest to the Carmelites because of its association with the medieval Carmelite saint, Simon Stock, a Kentish man.

In 1949 The Friars, as the house is called locally, came on the market. It was put up for sale by private treaty, and the Kentish Freemasons were interested in the possibility of acquiring it. Fr Elias Lynch, who knew 'everyone' in Kent, was approached by the Provincial Grand Master, who told him that if the Carmelites were in a position to make a bid for their ancient house, the Masons would be willing to withdraw. Which is what happened. The money was raised, every province of the Carmelite order contributing.

It was announced that the restored friary was to become an international house of higher studies for priest-members of the Order. The house was to be, for an indefinite time, directly subject to the Prior General of the Order, in Rome, Fr Elias's youngest

brother, Dr Kilian Lynch. The General appointed as the first prior
of the restored monastery his elder brother, Fr Malachy Lynch.
At first glance this may seem to have been a very nepotistic way
of proceeding; but there was some justification for it. Many of
the buildings at The Friars were in a state of great dilapidation;
an extensive and costly programme of repair would have to be
embarked on, and it would also be necessary to build a new
church. Fr Malachy was a dynamic personality, with a great gift for
fund-raising. All the same, I have always thought that his appointment as prior was a mistake. He was not really what in the religious
life is called a good community man; he was a visionary, a dreamer,
a builder of castles in the air, a man of mercurial temperament, as
changeable as the wind. Certainly he accomplished great things at
Aylesford, but some costly and unwise decisions were made, which
have proved an embarrassment to his successors. He had been a
great success in Wales, where he had built a beautiful small church
and priory at Lampeter, and he had a great understanding of and
sympathy with the Welsh people and their history and traditions. In
England he was less at home. I believe that Fr Elias Lynch would
have been a better choice as prior; but perhaps it was felt that the
Order's English finances would have been less competently administered if placed in other hands than his.

The recovery of the friary at Aylesford was given a great deal of
publicity in the national press. It was the first ancient religious
house in England to be repeopled by the Order that built it.
(Buckfast Abbey was originally Cistercian, but had been rebuilt
and resettled by Benedictines.) The restoration of this house of
religion caught the public imagination, and people began to visit it
in increasing numbers. Fr Malachy had quickly sensed that it
could be developed as a popular Marian shrine, and no more was
heard of the house of higher studies.

Repairs to the buildings were put in hand at once, and with
the number of pilgrims and visitors increasing rapidly it became
necessary to consider the question of building a new church. Mr
Adrian Gilbert Scott, a member of the distinguished architectural
family, offered his services, and his offer was accepted. He set to
work, and submitted, as a preliminary suggestion, a design not for a
church, but for a setting for the open-air worship of very large
congregations. By that time it was realized that summer congre-

gations on Sundays and festivals might well number up to three
thousand people, so that to contain them a church as big as
Westminster Cathedral would be needed. Even Fr Malachy, an
enthusiastic planner if ever there was one, felt that that would be
too big a project to embark on, at any rate for the moment. Adrian
Scott's first design was for an open-air altar, to be sited in front of
the magnificent copper-beech tree at the further end of the lawn in
front of the house. Underneath the altar there would be a crypt,
which would enshrine the reliquary containing the skull of Saint
Simon Stock. The question of what kind of church to build could be
shelved for the moment, so as to allow of a more pondered decision
later on.

At first Fr Malachy was delighted with Mr Scott's design; but he
soon decided that something bigger was required. After a visit to
the shrine of our Lady at Fatima he decided that what was wanted
at Aylesford was a large paved piazza, as at the famous Portuguese
shrine. To make way for this the lawn had to go; and the altar was
now planned to be placed on a raised and partly covered sanctuary
in front of the copper-beech tree.

For the time being, while the shrine was building, the large
hall on the first floor of the house, the very hall that had so
impressed the Kentish Freemasons, was converted into a chapel for
the community's worship. This hall had been the Earl of Aylesford's
drawing-room and music room; later it had served as his reception
room, with, at the east end, a small throne of state on a dais,
beneath a hanging tester. The throne, which had been removed
some years before, when the then earl sold the property, was now
replaced by an altar – the tester had been retained – and at the
corners of the dais were placed four gilded Venetian lamps on
poles, the gift of Fr Elias Lynch. The long and lofty apartment had
been extensively restored by the last secular owner after it had
been gutted by fire in 1929. It was well lit by Gothic windows on
either side, and made a splendid chapel, able to seat three hundred
people.

Mr Scott had now submitted a new plan for the open-air
sanctuary, but Fr Malachy was still not satisfied. In his next plan a
large roofed-in chapel was added, to the left of the sanctuary, its
main purpose being to house the relic of the saint.

At this point a young, recently qualified architect, John Jacques, came forward, unsolicited, with a design for a large temporary church of laminated wood. This, he said, would hold three thousand people, and would last for fifty years, by the end of which time the purpose and future of the priory would be more clearly seen. The cost of this temporary, wooden church would have been only £20,000. The idea was original, and the design pleasing. But it was not accepted. Perhaps Scott had already been commissioned.

When the shrine, as the complex of buildings that eventually arose, was called, it comprised the partially covered-in sanctuary, a chapel for the relic, a chapel of Saint Joseph, a small chapel dedicated to Saint Anne which, when its mural decorations were completed, looked more like Queen Victoria's boudoir than anything else, and a choir chapel for the community's daily worship. Pevsner's *The Buildings of Kent* gives the Aylesford shrine a very caustic notice. Other professional judgements have been no more favourable.

If the shrine must be considered an architectural failure, Fr Malachy's plans for its embellishment were more successful. The ceramic murals by the Polish artist Adam Kossowski are impressive, especially the huge golden angels on the walls to left and right of the altar, and the panel depicting the saints of the Carmelite Order behind the altar in the eastern transept of the relic chapel. Kossowski was really the discovery of the sculptor Philip Lindsey Clark, who recommended him to Fr Malachy. Kossowski's style is 'modern', yet with more than a hint of its origins in Polish folk-art. His rosary 'stations' in the garden behind the shrine at Aylesford are especially pleasing, I think. He seems to me a major artist; I do not understand why his work, which is to be seen also at Downside Abbey and other churches, and on a number of public buildings, has not attracted more attention.

Fr Malachy Lynch was one of the great religious beggars of the present century. He was quite shameless about this, and with justification; for, as he used to remind us in the talks that he gave at the weekly conventual chapter, the Carmelites are by origin a mendicant order. He really did trust in Providence, and practised the virtue of Magnificence, to which it belongs, Saint Thomas Aquinas tells us, to spend largely in the pursuit of noble objects. Providence, he believed, would, through the intercession of our Lady and Saint Joseph, provide for all the community's financial

needs. To raise funds for the restoration of the priory and the
building of the shrine he issued shares in what he called 'Our
Lady's Company': shares which were unredeemable and paid no
interest. The idea caught on, and the money came pouring in.
When asking for huge bank loans and overdrafts to pay for all the
work that was going on, he would astonish bank managers by
naming the Blessed Virgin as guarantor. It worked; but no doubt
the bank managers knew that a major religious order could not
default. Or if it did, that the Holy See would bale it out; as
happened with Abbot Aelred Carlyle's abbey of Saint Samson on
Caldey Island in 1928.

My novitiate at Aylesford passed without incident. As I was
already in solemn vows of religion it was simply a matter of my
renewing them in the Carmelite context. I was then free to complete my studies for the priesthood, which were nearly finished. For
this purpose I was sent to the Collegio Sant' Alberto, the Carmelite
international house of studies in Rome. I was there for six months,
and did not much enjoy it. The diet was insufficient for a
northerner, or at any rate for this northerner; and noise in the
streets at night made sleep impossible, or nearly so. And the
climate was trying both in winter and summer. When I left I had no
wish to see Rome again, and in fact I have never been back.
However, there is a certain satisfaction in having been able to
witness the dying splendours of papal Rome, before the destruction
of the ancient liturgy of the Roman church and the inauguration of
paupers' funerals for Popes.

Having now completed my studies, I was free to return to
England at the beginning of June 1954. Not long before I was due
to leave I received an invitation from Fr Desmond Chute, who for
many years had been living in Rapallo. Mary Gill had told him that
I was in Rome, and he wrote to tell me that he would shortly be in
Rome himself, and to ask me if I would care to join him one day in
a little excursion to Tuscany, to see some of the cathedrals there. I
wrote back at once to accept this kind invitation.

Desmond Chute was a man of high culture, an aesthete. He was
ordained on his patrimony – his family owned the Prince's Theatre
in Bristol – and poor health had led to his living in Italy, where
the climate suited him. In earlier days, when he had been Eric
Gill's right-hand-man at Ditchling, he had made many beautiful

paintings, etchings, and wood-engravings. But failing eyesight had brought to an end for him such work as this. After he had settled in Rapallo he had become a friend of Ezra and Dorothy Pound, and Olga Rudge; also of Max Beerbohm, whom he knew rather less well. At his house, the Villa San Rafaele, Father Chute would sometimes play on the piano the sonatas of Mozart and Pergolesi, and Olga Rudge would accompany him on her violin. During the war he had a difficult time, and was interned by the Germans, though under very humane conditions. When he was released he returned to Rapallo and moved into his final home, the Villa San Tomaso Moro. His health had deteriorated still further, but a variety of studies occupied his mind, and he had many tasks in hand, among them his never to be completed book on Eric Gill.

When I met Fr Chute in Rome, in the early summer of 1954, he was fifty-nine, a tall, impressive, bearded figure. By the standards of Britain it was an uncomfortably hot day, yet he emerged from his hotel wearing over his cassock a heavy priest's cloak. When he was seated in the front of his little car, his Italian chauffeur-valet placed over his knees a heavy rug, and then went back into the hotel. He emerged again a few minutes later with a hot-water bottle, which he placed under the rug on the Father's knees. Fr Chute had planned for my entertainment a tour of Tuscan cathedrals. These splendid churches, famous for their beautiful Cosmati pavements, are set in very small towns, villages almost. Fr Chute knew them all intimately. Today they have mostly lost their cathedral status; many of these tiny bishoprics having now been abolished.

Everywhere we stopped, Don Desmondo achieved a marked effect. Children ran to greet him; shopkeepers and innkeepers bowed low, almost to the ground; women kissed his hand. All this went a good deal beyond the normal respect for the clergy that was still common in rural Italy. These simple people seemed to take him, in spite of his plain black vesture, for some kind of prince of the church. With his great height, his impressive beard, and his commanding presence, he certainly looked the part. But I like to think that these gestures of respect were a spontaneous recognition of holiness; for Desmond Chute was a holy priest. Little known in England, he has nevertheless been described as one of the great priests of this century.

Altogether, we had a splendid day in Tuscany. Back in Rome in
the evening his last act, before we parted, was to buy a large and
expensive bouquet of flowers which he instructed me to place
before the altar of our Lady in the chapel of the Collegio Sant'
Alberto.

I never saw him again. Desmond Chute died peacefully on 14th
September, Holy Cross Day, 1962, at the age of sixty-seven. Ezra
Pound, no friend to the clergy, was at his funeral.

CHAPTER NINE

At Odds With The Red Hat

ON 18th July, 1954 I was ordained priest at Aylesford, the first priest to be ordained there since the Reformation, and was assigned to the Aylesford community. I was to spend the next fourteen years there, an unusually long time for a friar to remain in one place. This was fortunate for me; at that time none of our other houses could have offered such varied and interesting work. My orientation had always been monastic, and I had never thought that I was cut out to be a parish priest, or even an assistant curate. Still, I have always enjoyed the occasional spells of parish duty that have come my way; for one thing, they keep one in touch with the 'ordinary' people. In 1954 the Order had three parishes in Kent and three in Wales; today, 1991, it has one parish in Kent, one in Wales, and one in south-east London. In 1954 it had also a school for boys at Llandeilo, in Carmarthenshire, and a training college for late vocations to the priesthood at Aberystwyth. Both schools have since been given up.

At Aylesford the fathers took it in turns to help in neighbouring parishes at weekends. These parishes were chiefly the English Martyrs' at Strood and Saint Francis's, Maidstone; occasionally one helped out at West Malling, Chatham, or Sheerness. At Maidstone one often said Mass in the prison, where the chief Mass server was a baronet, Sir George. He was a charming man, and had been committed for a period of years on account of some piece of financial misjudgement; or so one understood. Less frequently one said Mass for the Catholic inmates at the original Borstal institution, at Borstal, near Rochester. Here the congregation was inclined to be restive, if not refractory, and had to be kept in order by its surveillant. The men in Maidstone Gaol were a much more amenable lot.

Soon I was asked to take on work with the Carmelite Third
Order, or tertiaries. In the 1950s the principal Third Order groups
were in London, Birmingham, Manchester, and Blackburn. The
Birmingham chapter met once a month, on a Saturday afternoon, in
Saint Chad's Cathedral, one of Pugin's finest churches. I usually
stayed the night at Solihull, where I enjoyed the hospitality of
two ladies, Olive and Marion Swingler, who ran a country club
in a magnificent old Regency house. They were great friends
and supporters of the Order, and their two other sisters were
founder-members of our Carmelite secular Institute, The Leaven.
On another weekend each month I had to go to Manchester, and
then on to Blackburn, returning to Aylesford on the Monday. There
were two groups of tertiaries in London; one met at the church of
the Assumption, in Warwick Street, near Piccadilly Circus, the
other in the Belgian church in Camden Town. These two groups
were under Fr Malachy's direction, but as he was quite often
unwell, I had sometimes to take care of them also. I enjoyed this
work; at the meetings one said Mass or officiated at Benediction,
and gave the tertiaries a talk on some aspect of Carmelite tradition
and spirituality. The tertiaries were good people, loyal to the Order,
and very supportive.

At Aylesford my first task was to organize a library for the
priory. It was a few years before any funds at all were made
available for this purpose, and then they were meagre. Nevertheless, progress was made. During my novitiate there had been
barely three hundred books in the house, and those mostly of little
interest. There was not even a room set apart for the library. A
room was duly designated, a pleasant room, of moderate size, on
the first floor, and overlooking the lawn, which had not yet been
replaced by the piazza. Over the next few years the contents of the
library increased quickly. We received many gifts of books, and a
few modest bequests of books from secular priests who had died.
And after we had started our magazine, the *Aylesford Review*, the
library gained perhaps about a hundred new books each year at
no cost, in the form of review copies, many of which had been
specifically requested by the editor on account of their suitability
for an ecclesiastical library.

The Prior General, Dr Kilian Lynch, had instructed me to start
this magazine. It was intended to be a small quarterly publication,

providing suitable reading for our tertiaries and other friends of the Order. The first number appeared in the autumn of 1955, its cover, but the cover only, being printed at our newly set up small printing office, Saint Albert's Press. Under the magazine's title, in Berthold Wolpe's Albertus typeface (how appropriate), the cover held the first page of the first article, set in Gill's Perpetua, opening with a Gill Floriated initial letter. The text was set with an uneven righthand edge, and thus conformed to the best Ditchling-Pigotts principles. I still think it a rather pleasing design. The rest of the magazine was printed elsewhere in Stanley Morison's Times New Roman, a first-rate typeface for newspapers and magazines, but unsuitable for bookwork: as too few publishers realize.

This first number of the *Aylesford Review* met with no acclaim; in fact, it fell flat. Very few of the thousand or so potential readers whom we had hoped to interest responded. By and large it seemed that our tertiaries were not great readers. Father Malachy, indeed, said that there was no need at all for such a magazine, since the Order's associates and friends were perfectly content with his quarterly *Pilgrims' News Letter*, which was distributed free of charge to all who cared to receive it. Perhaps he was right.

The second number, which was enlarged from twelve to twenty pages, was no more successful, nor was the third. At that point the Prior General authorized me to carry on the magazine as best I could, with the proviso that no financial aid would be forthcoming.

If the magazine were to continue, some kind of reorien- tation seemed called for. In the autumn of 1956 I attended a conference in London, convened by the editor of *Blackfriars*, on 'The Purpose of a Review'. The principal speakers were Archbishop David Mathew, Mr Alan Pryce-Jones (editor of the *Times Literary Supplement*), and Dr Frank Sheed (of the publishing house of Sheed and Ward). There were also contributions from Miss Rose Macaulay and her sister, Dr Letitia Fairfield. The editorial in the next number of the *Aylesford Review* discussed some of the ideas put forward at this conference. 'Naturally,' it said, 'a review which represents a society or organiz- ation, whether religious or secular, cannot be as outspoken as one which is the mouthpiece of an individual.' In breach of this principle the *Aylesford Review* was some years later to print a number of articles on topics of the day that were highly contro- versial. For instance, in the 1960s it published articles on the

Official Secrets Trial, corruption in the police, the seeming con-
nivance of the police in an attempt to murder Sir Oswald Mosley,
and on the Profumo and Stephen Ward scandal.

At the Official Secrets Trial at the Old Bailey in 1962 six
members of the Committee of One Hundred who had attempted
a peaceful protest-infiltration of the American air base at
Wethersfield, in East Anglia, were prosecuted under the Official
Secrets Act. None of the six was accused of spying or of betraying
official secrets, yet all were sentenced to terms of imprisonment.
The five men received sentences of eighteen months; the one
woman, Mrs Helen Allegranza, twelve months.

In court the defence witnesses were shamefully bullied and
harried. One of them, Archbishop Roberts, of the Society of Jesus,
a former Archbishop of Bombay, was barred by the Judge from
giving evidence, on the grounds that the Court was not interested in
the morality of the accused's actions. Questions put for the defence
to the distinguished scientist Sir Robert Watson-Watt were ruled
out of order. Helen Allegranza died soon after her release from
prison. In April 1963 the *Aylesford Review* published an appreciation of her that had been written and signed by her five fellow-
prisoners. Afterwards I received this message from Archbishop
Roberts.

114 Mount Street
London W1
May 22nd '63

Dear Reverend Father,

I'm much ashamed to put off so long thanking you for the Review
containing your reference to Helen Allegranza. It was most kind and
thoughtful of you to send the earlier issue to the 'Old Bailey' prisoners.

You have anticipated the *'Pacem in terris'** approach, but may have to
wait for your reward. The halo will last much longer than a red hat!

Devotedly yours in Xto,

+ T.D. Roberts, S.J.

[*Pacem in terris': the opening words of an encyclical letter of Pope John
XXIII.]

An article in the winter number of 1963-'64, 'After the Denning
Report', was described in the Socialist weekly *Tribune* as 'most

acute and charitable'; in the *New Statesman* a writer described it as 'a priest's assault on the Denning Report'. This was followed, in the spring number, by a four-page review-article on Ludovic Kennedy's book *The Trial of Stephen Ward*. The spring issue had already gone to press when the review copy of the book arrived, so the article had to be printed separately, and inserted as a four-page loose inset. It began by quoting Diana Mosley's comment, in her quarterly magazine *The European*, on Lord Denning's *Report* on the Ward-Profumo affair. 'Most of us', Lady Mosley said, 'could have written the thing with our eyes shut without the least trouble.' The writer of the *Aylesford Review* article asked why Stephen Ward had killed himself, and answered the question by saying that the Trial Judge's summing up had been a determining factor. The writer found that 'the most curious feature of Lord Denning's report was his eulogy of Lord Astor, a friend of Stephen Ward's who had dropped him when the trial came on, but was praised by Lord Denning for his charitable munificences, important business interests, and his famous stud of race-horses.' No such sympathetic interest, the writer went on, was shown by the learned Judge to the unhappy Stephen Ward. 'Yet one might have thought that if eulogies were to be bestowed on Stephen Ward's upper-class associates, a word or two of compassion might have been found for Dr Ward himself.'

Some of the humbler people associated with the Stephen Ward *milieu* had their careers shattered and their lives seriously upset. Some, indeed, were destroyed: among them John Hamilton-Marshall, a young man who, after the affair was over, tried hard to extricate himself. After the trial of Stephen Ward he left London, and lived for a time on a barge on the River Medway, near Rochester. While there John got himself a job at Reed's paper-mills at Aylesford, where he sometimes came to see me at the priory. He had suffered something of a mental breakdown, and from then on was occasionally a voluntary patient in mental hospitals. He tried hard to rehabilitate himself, and eventually he held for some time a good position as a farm manager in Norfolk. But he was never quite cured, and eventually died of an overdose: possibly an accident. There was much good in John. I wish he had been able to survive.

About the same time, I met Christine Keeler in a London hospital where we were each visiting a mutual friend. I was as

much impressed by her good manners and natural dignity as by her
beauty, and we have remained good friends since.

All things considered, it seems strange that these controversial
articles in the *Aylesford Review* drew no comment from my
superiors; but I fancy that neither the Prior nor the Prior General,
when he was present, ever actually read the magazine. Fr Malachy
did not approve of it; Fr Kilian read little except theology. However, two years later, in 1966, a quite different kind of contribution
got the editor into hot water. Two elderly ladies living in the friary
guesthouse complained to the General, who was on an informal
visit to Aylesford, about a review in the magazine of a novel of the
day by a well respected writer. The review, by Rachel Attwater, was
favourable, so they borrowed a copy of the book from the Maidstone
public library. They claimed to have been greatly shocked by it.
The General did not bother to read the book himself, but sent for
the editor and gave him a sharp dressing-down. In addition, he said
that an editorial board would have to be set up, so as to prevent
future incidents of this kind. In the event, however, the board
never met. Its five members lived far apart, most of them at a
considerable distance from Aylesford; they showed no inclination
to meet, and it had never been specified who was to convene their
meetings.

In 1963 and 1964 there had been rather a concentration in the
Review of articles on public affairs and questions of social justice;
but as it developed it became mainly a literary magazine, with
some emphasis on theology and sociology. When the magazine was
started one of my hopes had been to publish work by young
aspiring writers. Among those whose early work we printed were
Angela Carter, Frances Horovitz, Paul Roche, Penelope Shuttle,
D.M. Thomas, and Michael Horovitz. The first number had a poem
by Muriel Spark, who was then living in a cottage in the grounds of
Allington Castle, writing her first novel, *The Comforters*. Looking through the bound volumes of the magazine, which ceased
publication in 1968, I notice contributions from Fleur Adcock,
John Gawsworth, Elizabeth Jennings, Thomas Merton, George – D.
Painter, Stevie Smith, Sylvia Townsend Warner, Henry Williamson,
and Colin Wilson. Not a bad range of contemporary talent.

Aylesford is easy of access from London; soon some of the
writers and artists contributing to the *Review* began using the priory

guesthouse as a weekend meeting place. Among the younger writers and artists who came to stay were Frances Horovitz and her friend Jane Percival, and Nicola Wood, who had been at the Royal College of Art with Jane.

Other visitors were Michael Hastings, and the photographer Oswald Jones. The youngest of the group was Penelope Shuttle, who had begun publishing her poems in the *Aylesford Review* almost as soon as she had left school. Among others who came, but less frequently, were Michael Horovitz and Colin Wilson. Nicola Wood has for the last quarter of a century been living in California, where she is well known as a painter. An article in a recent issue of the American magazine *Car Collector* says that 'Wood is driven, devoted, and extremely passionate, with an eye for classical art and a sincere determination to preserve the teachings of the Renaissance masters. Yet this ardent English painter has a wonderfully devilish love for the outlandish, the extreme and the defiant.'

There were also some older writers, among them Henry Williamson, on whose life and work we had published a special number of the *Review* in 1955. Another, though he was younger than Williamson, was the novelist Gabriel Fielding (in private life Dr Alan Barnsley), who lived in Maidstone. In 1960 he left with his wife and family for the United States, where he embarked on a brilliant academic career. His novel *The Birthday King* was published in 1962, and received very high acclaim. I remember Alan Barnsley as a man so over-brimming with life that he made the rest of us seem like half-expired electric batteries.

Another highly valued contributor to the *Aylesford Review* was the historian and novelist Alan Neame, surely one of the 'refined'st Witts of the Age', who was then living at Fisher Street, near Faversham. He has since removed to his parents' former home, Trafalgar House, built in the year of the battle, at Selling, where he has concentrated on his work as a translator from ancient and modern languages, and as a leading historian of his native county of Kent. I have profited much from his friendship, and from his timely admonitions and advice.

In the course of the *Review*'s thirteen years' existence we published a few special numbers devoted to the consideration of the life and work of writers whose work we thought was too little known or appreciated. These included Arthur Machen, Henry

Williamson, Elizabeth Myers, John Gray, and the French writer
Joseph Delteil. The number on Delteil contained two different
articles on him by Henry Miller, one in English, the other in
French.

The Henry Williamson number, which appeared in 1957, had
articles by William Gore Allen, Malcolm Elwin, and George D.
Painter, with a specially written article by Williamson himself. At
this time he was still much disprized on account of his pre-war
support of the policies of national regeneration advocated by Sir
Oswald Mosley, to whom he had remained loyal throughout the war
and after.

It was Henry Williamson who brought the *avant garde* novelist
Ann Quin to Aylesford, at the time of the great success, in 1964, of
her first novel, *Berg*. Ann, alas, was found drowned off the coast at
Brighton in the summer of 1973. Another friend who found life
increasingly a strain was Zahra Rayman, whom I first met, in 1961,
in Peter Russell's bookshop in D'Arblay Street, Soho. She was then
twenty-six. She had been born in Kashmir, and was a Muslim, but
had been educated at a Catholic convent-school in Lahore. When
I met her she was working as a model at the Royal College of
Art, and was herself a painter; she was hoping to find work as
a part-time teacher of Pakistani children with English-language
difficulties. How or why she had come to England I do not know;
the climate tried her greatly, and she had to spend a lot of time in
hospital. Zahra was a woman of extraordinary beauty and great
nobility of character. She had a refined aesthetic sense, and looked
quite dazzlingly distinguished in either eastern or western dress.
She was a very gentle and compassionate person, yet in a photograph of her taken by the professional photographer Ida Karr she
looks quite *farouche*. The camera had caught an aspect of her that
was not readily apparent; in a letter which she wrote to me in 1967
she says: 'Basically there's a lot of the primitive tribal hillswoman
in me.' She had a large front room in a house in the Cromwell
Road, in London, and the noise of the all-night traffic prevented
her from sleeping: it was this that led to her death. I miss her
greatly; and Ann Quin too, about whom I have written in my book
Like Black Swans.

Henry Williamson became very fond of the priory at Aylesford,
and enjoyed being with the little group of writers and artists whom

he met there. He also appreciated, as we all did, the hospitality which we often received, on Saturday or Sunday evenings, at Wickham Lodge, the home of our community's doctor, Eustace Edmonds, and his wife Betty. Dr Edmonds was a man of wide culture and great sensibility. He had a profound knowledge and understanding of the seventeenth century metaphysical poets, and of the Cambridge Platonists, whose works, often in first or contemporary editions, adorned his library. Henry Williamson had a special regard for him.

To go back a little in the history of the revived Aylesford Priory, in 1955 Fr Malachy's second term of office as Prior came to an end. The time had come for him to stand down. The priory was still directly subject to the General of the Order, who had the right of appointment. News of this was awaited with some anxiety. When it came, there was a general feeling of surprise. The nomination had gone to a friar who was a total stranger to most of us: Fr Patrick Russell, an Irish priest who had just retired from the office of Provincial Prior of the Order's New York province. Fr Russell, who contrived somehow, but quite typically, to arrive at Aylesbury (in Buckinghamshire) instead of Aylesford, was a tall, distinguished looking man, aged about sixty. He had a disarming simplicity of manner that concealed a shrewd intelligence. Thus he would express surprise at quite ordinary things that he was told, his favoured expression of surprise being the words: "Saint Anthony!" He was once heard to say to someone at Dublin airport who had told him where he could buy a packet of cigarettes: "Thank you. How wonderful! Whoever would have thought of that!" When conducting a church service he once announced the recitation of the rosary in these words: "The Five Joyful – no, Sorrowful – I mean Glorious Mysteries of the Most Holy Rosary. First mystery, the Nativity." This is such an amazing muddle that any attempt to elucidate it could only make matters worse.

Fr Russell was a cultivated man, and a gentleman. He was a good conversationalist, and had a nice sense of humour. As a religious superior he had the great merit, not always found in superiors, of taking a real interest in his community and its individual members, their work, activities, and personal well-being. He had not been long at Aylesford, however, before it became clear that his was a stop-gap or interim appointment only;

for just one year, after which Fr Malachy would be canonically eligible for reappointment. In fact, when Prior Russell arrived, Fr Malachy did not even bother to move to another house of the Order, as is the wise custom with outgoing priors, but remained firmly in place. The pretext for this was that he was needed at The Friars to continue to superintend the building of the shrine, which was now in progress; but he could have done this just as well from Allington Castle, which was only two miles away, or even from Faversham.

Another of the qualities of the good religious superior is that he or she always comes to the aid of any of their subjects who are in any kind of trouble, even if they are at fault. Fr Russell soon had occasion to show that he possessed this quality. I had kept up my membership of the PAX Society, and in fact was an active member. My thoughts on the morality of war had developed. In 1941 Pope Pius XII had spoken of weapons of war 'which tend to go beyond every moral norm', and had condemned the use of such weapons. (He was speaking of some of the 'conventional' weapons of the pre-nuclear era.) Now, in the 1950s, we were faced with the existence of nuclear weapons which did unquestionably go beyond every moral norm.

At the 1955 annual general meeting in London of the Catholic Truth Society, a propagandist publishing enterprise, Cardinal Griffin, the Society's president, addressed its members on this subject. The Cardinal seemed to have no misgivings about the morality of modern warfare, and took the usual 'Establishment' line that such matters were best left to the Government to decide, because it alone had access to all the facts; and that to suggest otherwise was unpatriotic. After alluding in a general way to the rights of conscience, the Cardinal expressed concern over certain publications discussing these matters, which were appearing 'ostensibly from Catholic sources, but without any form of true ecclesiastical authority . . . with quotations lifted quite out of their context from statements made by Popes and continental theologians.' I rather liked the reference to continental theologians. Those foreigners, you know!

These remarks were obviously aimed at PAX; but since he had not named the Society, nor any particular writer or publication, they could not really be challenged. Nor was it clear where the writers of these unspecified pamphlets or articles were supposed to have gone wrong.

At about this time the ÇTS published a sixpenny pamphlet, *Peace and War*, by the Reverend G.J. McGillivray, DD. This pamphlet so distorted and travestied the position of Catholic pacifists and war-resisters that I was moved to write a letter of complaint to the Cardinal. At about the same time Dr McGillivray's pamphlet was severely criticized in the *Pax Bulletin*. To these criticisms Dr McGillivray made no reply; and when he was invited to defend his position in either a public debate or a private discussion, he declined the invitation.

I received from the Cardinal a brief reply to my letter to him. In it he informed me of the existence in this country of the 'official' international Catholic peace movement, Pax Christi. Pax Christi was a recent importation (from the Continent!), and no one seemed to have heard of it. Its activities, if there had been any, had attracted little or no attention. In his letter to me the Cardinal made no reference to Dr McGillivray or his pamphlet: the matter on which I had written to him. PAX's Committee now decided that a pamphlet should be prepared setting out and vindicating the principles on which the Society was based, and that it should be offered to the CTS for publication as a companion or supplement to Dr McGillivray's pamphlet. The writing of this proposed pamphlet was assigned to a leading PAX member, Mr Thomas Whitton, a former Anglican clergyman.

In August the general secretary of the CTS, a Mr Rittner, wrote to tell me that Mr Whitton's pamphlet had not been accepted for publication. In acknowledging his letter I told him that PAX would now make its own arrangements for the publication of Mr Whitton's essay. This evidently caused him some alarm, with the result that towards the end of September Prior Russell received a letter from the Roman Catholic Bishop of Southwark, in whose diocese Aylesford lay, saying that he had heard that I was intending to print and publish at Saint Albert's Press a pamphlet on Catholic pacifism which had been rejected by the Catholic Truth Society.

The Bishop could have had this erroneous information from the CTS only. There had never been any question of Mr Whitton's pamphlet being printed at Aylesford. When challenged about this Mr Rittner admitted that it was himself who had brought the matter to the Bishop's attention. My denial of any such intent seemed to put an end to the matter as far as the Bishop was concerned.

But a little later the matter came alive again, in a different form. After breakfast at The Friars one morning Fr Russell, assisted by two other priests, was opening the priory's post. Fr Malachy's newsletter always had a big response from its readers, and at peak times it took two or three men to deal with it. All of a sudden the two other fathers were astonished to hear Fr Russell exclaim: "Saint Anthony! Brocard is in trouble with the Red Hat." The letter he had just opened had nothing to do with Fr Malachy's appeal for funds, but was from the Bishop of Southwark, who enclosed with it a letter he had received from his metropolitan, the Archbishop of Westminster. Cardinal Griffin began by reminding his suffragan that he, the Cardinal, had been worried for some time about what he called 'the Pax organisation', most of whose members, he slyly observed, lived in the diocese of Southwark. (This was pure fantasy.) PAX, he said, had criticized the Hierarchy 'from time to time' – a major offence, evidently – and was now 'in open warfare' with the Catholic Truth Society. He himself had been openly attacked in the last number of the PAX Bulletin.

This apparently referred to an article, 'The Hydrogen Bomb and Sin', which said that Cardinal Griffin and the Archbishop of York (Dr Garbett) had both denounced the H-bomb as evil, 'yet at the same time they have both claimed that we should make it for expediency's sake.' 'Since when', the writer asked, 'has it been lawful for a Christian to make use of an evil thing for a good end?'

In his letter to the Bishop the Cardinal said that most of the people in PAX were 'a bit cracked'; there was, however, a Carmelite at Aylesford who was supporting the movement. 'He already knows my views, but I see that he spoke at their last Annual General Meeting.' Perhaps the Bishop would care to discuss the matter with the Prior of Aylesford?

What was there, one might ask, to discuss? The priest in question had certainly done nothing wrong in giving a talk at a PAX meeting on Josef Metzger, a German pacifist priest who had been executed under the Hitler régime.

In January 1956 a scholastic disputation, in strict medieval form, was held by the Dominican Fathers, on the invitation of the

National Peace Council, at Caxton Hall, Westminster, and was broadcast on the Third Programme of the BBC. The motion proposed for debate affirmed that, subject to certain precautions and safeguards, the use of nuclear weapons of war is morally permissible. The motion was proposed and defended by Fr Columba Ryan, and opposed by Fr Laurence Bright, a former nuclear physicist. After an hour or so of dispassionate syllogistic argument the proponent had to surrender, and to concede that the objector to the motion had shown not only that the use of nuclear weapons was totally immoral, but also that their manufacture and retention as a 'deterrent' was immoral.

Inspired by this, I wrote once again to the long-suffering Cardinal, inviting him to seek from the Holy See a formal condemnation of the conclusion arrived at in this debate. 'If this cannot be done,' I said, 'members of the PAX Society will see in this disputation, conducted by priests of position and standing, belonging to an Order whose members are specialists in the science of ethics, a vindication of all that they have been saying, not without distinguished theological backing, for many years past.'

Thinking to appease the Cardinal, the Bishop now sent an inquisitor, Dom Anselm Thatcher, the Abbot of Ramsgate, to Aylesford, to interrogate the supposed delinquent. The Prior was considerably startled by the news of this coming visitation; but once he had got over the shock, and had had time to reflect, he thought that probably I could not be convicted of anything worse than lecturing the Cardinal, and that nothing much was likely to happen. The Abbot duly arrived, and interviewed me with great politeness. He soon decided that I had committed no offence, and said that he would notify the Bishop accordingly. That was the end of the matter. Bernard Griffin was a churchman of modest talents. He had done well as an auxiliary bishop in the diocese of Birmingham, but he was not suited to higher office.

I look back on the time of Fr Patrick Russell's priorship as the all too brief golden age of the revived priory at Aylesford. Almost as soon as he had taken office tensions and anxieties in the community faded out, and life became less stressful. Fr Russell's short term of office was marked by a notable liturgical revival, whose principal feature was the Solemn Sung Vespers on Sunday afternoons, with cantors in copes, and the use of incense. The

singing was under the direction of Fr Bede Caine, a genial yet
irascible man with a splendid voice. Still remembered by some
older brethren is the High Mass that was celebrated on the feast of
Corpus Christi in June 1956, in the chapel that had once been the
Earl of Aylesford's hall of state. The singing on this occasion of the
sequence 'Lauda, Sion, Salvatorem' reached an astonishing degree
of perfection. The service was broadcast by the BBC, and happily
there is a recording of it.

A valuable member of the community a lttle later was Leonard
Love, a priest from the Order's New York province, a man of
unmistakable goodness, who was with us for some years as bursar.
As such he was responsible for the welfare of the lay workers in our
employment, of whom there were several while the reconstruction
of the priory was going on. Fr Malachy, who was still prior at this
point, was always generous in receiving and harbouring men, and
sometimes women, who were temporarily homeless, or otherwise
down on their luck, and in helping them to get back onto their feet.
One day a very broken-down looking young man, bearded, and of
Asian appearance, arrived at the priory seeking help. He was
destitute, or very near it, and some priest in London had told him:
"Go and see Fr Lynch at Aylesford." The name of this refugee was
Edward Morris. Fr Malachy handed him over to Fr Leonard, who
put him to work in our carpenters' workshop, where two or three
laybrothers worked under the direction of Mr Charles Bodiam, a
master carpenter and joiner. Under his instruction, Morris (as he
liked to be called by his family and friends) got on very well,
and became a useful and skilled worker. After a year or so he
left, completely rehabilitated, and went back to London, where he
became an expert and successful dealer in rare books and prints,
with a shop in Museum Street, which he ran in partnership with the
girl whom he had married, who was a knowledgeable as himself, if
not more so.

Morris was always something of a mystery. One heard, and
apparently it was the truth, or something like it, that he was an
Afghan prince, and the hereditary captain of the bodyguard of
the Tsar of All the Russias. He was a delightful man, always
happy in the company of his friends. His death at quite an early
age was much regretted by all who knew him, among them
Henry Williamson, who greatly enjoyed meeting him at our annual

Aylesford Review reunions at Spode House, the Dominican conference centre in the Midlands.

Fr Russell's term of office as prior proved to be of even shorter duration than we had expected. He had been with us barely six months when the Prior General sent him on a bizarre mission as chaperon to a party of Portuguese Carmelite nuns who were travelling from Lisbon to Kenya, to make a new foundation there. He was away for about three months. On his return from Afric's sunny clime it was winter in England. There was snow everywhere, and chill winds blew through the open cloister at The Friars through which the community had to walk to reach the new refectory that Fr Malachy had built. Fr Russell suffered greatly from the cold. The winter in East Kent is always unpleasant, and it must have been especially so for someone who had been accustomed to the central heating in American houses. He did not complain; but his condition was pitiful to see. He had not been back a week when he suffered a severe heart attack, and was removed to hospital. He recovered; but that was the end of his brief, and much appreciated, priorship. His last years were spent at Terenure College, outside Dublin, where conditions were less spartan.

CHAPTER TEN

Friendship, Peculiar Boon of Heaven

In 1959 Dr Kilian Lynch's second term of office as Prior General, completing twelve years in all, came to an end. He had accomplished a great work for the Order. After the war he had raised large sums of money to help a number of small Italian friaries which the war had almost bankrupted, through damage caused to buildings and other factors; but perhaps his best memorial is the Carmelite Institute in Rome which he founded as a centre of historical research, whose long line of learned publications, including the polyglot journal *Carmelus*, has placed all Carmelites in his debt. But he failed to secure re-election, for a third term, as was then possible (but is no longer so today).

The General Chapter of 1959 elected another American to succeed Dr Lynch, Fr Kilian Healy, a professor of theology in the Collegio Sant' Alberto. One of the new General's first acts was to nominate his predecessor to succeed Fr Malachy Lynch, whose term of office had finally run out, as Prior of Aylesford.

This time Fr Malachy did move out, and went to live at nearby Allington Castle; but he still remained in charge of the shrine at Aylesford, and the pilgrimages, until eventually a complete breakdown in health compelled him to give up. Whatever one may think about the architectural merits of the shrine at Aylesford, there can be no doubt that Fr Malachy had a wonderful gift for dealing with large crowds of people, making each one feel individually that he or she was welcome. In fact, he had an extraordinary rapport with the pilgrims and other visitors to the priory, and there was no one else who would have done this work so effectively and untiringly.

One day the new prior, Fr Kilian, told me that Fr Malachy needed the premises occupied by Saint Albert's Press in the new workshop block for conversion into a tea-room for pilgrims and tourists. The Press and its staff – one laybrother and two secular employees – would have to move to Saint Mary's College, our house of studies at Llandeilo, in Carmarthenshire. This operation, which was very costly, was carried out; but after two years there the Press had to be closed, because in Llandeilo we could get no jobbing work; at Aylesford it was the work done for outside customers that was a main factor in keeping both the Press itself and the *Aylesford Review* going. But our house at Llandeilo was well outside the little Welsh town, in which there were already three printers competing against each other.

At Aylesford we had done some quite creditable book printing. The first edition of Eleanor Farjeon's memoir of the novelist Elizabeth Myers had been printed on a folio Albion handpress, under the supervision of Edward Walters, who came with his wife and children for a short holiday during three successive summers. Two or three other small books we had printed on our Autovic powered press. At Llandeilo most of our work was done on a Wharfdale flat-bed powered press. For bookwork we mostly used Monotype, hired from Western Printing Services Ltd in Bristol. Wrenne Jarman's *Nymph, in thy Orisons* and Lady Margaret Sackville's *Quatrains* were carefully designed books of poetry, set, respectively, in Monotype Bembo and Eric Gill's Perpetua. Henry Williamson's chapter of autobiography, *In The Woods*, was set in Monotype Baskerville. This small book was Saint Albert's Press's bestseller. We printed one thousand copies, instead of our usual two to three hundred, and they sold out quickly. Henry generously forewent his royalties, which he donated to the support of the *Aylesford Review*.

When the Press closed down I was glad to be able to return to Aylesford. In Wales I always feel that I am in conquered territory; the clouds and mountains seem to increase the atmosphere of depression. In Scotland it is quite different; there there is a sense of surviving nationhood and a living culture.

By now Fr Malachy at Allington really was 'king of the castle', in charge as chaplain, and with no tiresome *confrères* to obstruct and bother him. True, he suffered some frustration at being unable to embark on any more ambitious schemes, such as his proposed 'City of Mary', to be built in the Castle grounds; indeed, he was sometimes heard to say of his brother at Aylesford, who was now his prior: "Father Kilian doesn't understand." And, of course, he didn't.

But as he aged Fr Malachy became less restless and agitated. The best picture of him, to my mind, better than any photograph, is the portrait painted during his last years by Mrs Freeman (the artist Mary Dudley Short). Two versions of this portrait exist, one large, one small; both are now in the priory at Aylesford. In these pictures the artist has caught the real Fr Malachy, a deeply spiritual man who had suffered by being promoted to positions of authority at too early an age, and retained in them for too long. At Allington he recovered his ancient wisdom and austere control, and was, indeed, a greatly loved man.

For many years the Castle was something of a liability, and not a few of the brethren thought that it ought to be sold. But for a time at least Fr Malachy's faith in its future seemed justified. It was popular as a retreat house. Even if its finances were precarious, the rents from the cottages in the grounds eased the situation; the conversion of an ancient timbered barn into six flats was a further help. It was Fr Malachy's belief that if retired people of private means wished to settle at Allington and do voluntary work for the Order, then they should pay handsomely for the privilege. And people did so. One of the two larger flats on the upper floor of the former barn was occupied for many years by one of Fr Malachy's staunchest supporters, Sheila Blaxter. Mrs Blaxter was an Irish lady of great charm and vivacity, and considerable vagueness of mind. Fr Malachy had never learned to drive a car, so one of her great services to him was to drive him in her powerful Bentley when he needed to go to London, or to Faversham to see his elder brother, Fr Elias, or on other missions. As she grew older her driving became increasingly erratic, so that even an excursion to Maidstone with her was apt to be hazardous. However, by that time Fr Malachy rarely went anywhere except on his daily afternoon visit to Aylesford; something he never missed until he became confined to his room.

Mrs Blaxter's flat was furnished with great elegance, in the Late Empire style. She loved to entertain, and her hospitality verged on the lavish. I remember once being driven by her to Bath, to see a mutual friend who was in hospital there; and how, after we had been to the hospital, I persuaded her to join me in a little pilgrimage to the tomb of William Beckford, in the cemetery adjoining Lansdown Tower, high up and overlooking the city of Bath. I think she had not previously heard of the Caliph of Fonthill; but she quite entered into the spirit of the occasion, and helped me to pluck a sprig of lilac to place on his tomb.

One of the smaller ground-floor flats in the former barn at Allington was leased to Archibald Colquhoun, the translator of the Count of Lampedusa's novel *Il Gattopardo*, Manzoni's *I Promessi Sposi*, and other Italian classics. Archie had a gentle, unaffected aristocracy of manner which perhaps owed something to breeding and something to the Benedictine *gravitas* of his education at Ampleforth. There had been sadness in his life – his marriage had ended unhappily, and he had not remarried – and he was a man of great reserve. When one got to know him he proved a good friend; he had a basic kindness and good humour, often expressed in a dry wit. In his younger days he had been a communist. When he was an officer in the Army during the war he had been a liaison officer with the Italian partisans. After a period of estrangement from the Church he found his way back, and finally made his home at Allington.

I once took my friend Mary Silverthorne to pay an afternoon call on Mr Colquhoun. He received us with his accustomed amiability, and asked us if we would care to partake of coffee. We said, yes please. He then disapppeared into what looked like a tiny cupboard, but was in fact his mini-kitchen. After some minutes he reappeared, bearing two coffee-cups, which he handed to us, saying: "I hope you like Turkish coffee?" We signified our assent. Expecting a rare and delicious beverage, we raised the cups, at which we had barely glanced, to our lips, and were astonished to find that we had each taken in a mouthful of what seemed to be solid coffee-grounds. Archie himself, meanwhile, was partaking of another cup. No comment was made by any of us. Mrs Silverthorne and myself often recall this incident, which at the time made great demands on our powers of self-control. That is the only occasion on which I have actually had to chew coffee.

Another friend whom I often saw was Erica Marx, the owner and director of The Hand and Flower Press at Aldington. Her parents were German Jews, but she had been born in England. Her father had been a very rich man; with the portion of his wealth that she inherited she was able to take up private-press printing, which she had learned in Paris. She was a generous woman, and used her wealth to support a number of good causes, one of them being the Beauchamp Lodge settlement in Paddington. She gave a number of rare volumes to our library at Aylesford, among them the magnificent folio edition of Saint Augustine's *De Civitate Dei* printed by the Bremer Press at Munich in the 1930s. She also made a generous gift of money to our own Saint Albert's Press for the purchase of type.

It was a curious trait in Erica's character that in spite of her wealth and many accomplishments she often seemed to prefer to take a lowly position rather than the prominent place which was hers by rights. I think she was a genuinely humble person. She knew 'everyone' in the worlds of writing, printing, and publishing, and was the friend of such people as Vita Sackville-West, Cyril Connolly, and T.S. Eliot. At a party which she gave in London, at the Dorchester Hotel, Mr Eliot was present, standing quietly at the back of the room, and I had the honour of being presented to him.

The 1950s brought me in touch with the Dickens scholar Leslie C. Staples, who became a much valued friend. What brought us together was my interest in that strange scholar and equivocal churchman, the Reverend Montague Summers. I was anxious to trace the missing manuscript of Summers's autobiography, *The Galanty Show*, and in response to an inquiry in the *Times Literary Supplement* it was Mr Staples who gave me the clue that enabled me to find it. And it was his help, together with that of Mr Timothy d'Arch Smith, that made possible the writing of my book *Montague Summers: A Memoir*, which was published pseudonymously, as by Joseph Jerome, by Cecil Woolf in 1956. Cecil was eager to publish *The Galanty Show*, but its author had died, in 1948, before he could revise it, and much editorial work had to be done on it. It did not appear until 1980; this was a most suitable year, however, because it was the centenary year of Summers's birth.

Leslie Staples, one of the few surviving people who had known Dr Summers at all well, was born in 1896, the son of a prosperous London tradesman. In 1909 he won as a school prize a copy of *Nicholas Nickleby*. It would not be too much to say that from that moment his greatest pleasure in life was the study and enjoyment of the works of Charles Dickens, and that it became his principal mission in life to serve and promote the interests of the Dickens Fellowship, of which he came to be elected President. For many years he was the editor of the Fellowship's magazine, *The Dickensian.*

Mr Staples lived in a picturesque, bow-windowed old house on the banks of the Regents Park Canal: Number Seven, Lyme Terrace, NW1. Here, in this peaceful backwater, he lived among his *Dickensiana*, and his splendid collection of the first editions, signed limited editions, and manuscripts of the works of Montague Summers, historian of witchcraft and demonology, and of the Restoration Drama and the Gothic Novel. During the late 1960s and the 1970s Leslie was much vexed and disappointed by continuing delay in the publication of *The Galanty Show*, whose manuscript, once it had been found, and the copyright in it, were bought by Erica Marx and presented to me as a gift. On 10th April, 1980 the following notice appeared in the 'In Memoriam' column of *The Times*, at the instance of Leslie Staples, Timothy d'Arch Smith, Devendra Varma (professor of English at Dalhousie University, Halifax, N.S.), and myself.

SUMMERS, MONTAGUE: 10th August, 1948
Scholar and Divine. Sometime of Trinity College, Oxford. Author of *The History of Witchcraft and Demonology*, *The Restoration Theatre*, *The Playhouse of Pepys*, *The Gothic Quest*, *The Galanty Show*. Editor of the Works of Aphra Behn, Congreve, Dryden, Otway, Shadwell, Wycherley; and of *The Supernatural Omnibus*. Translator of *The Glories of Mary* and *Malleus Maleficarum*. Principal Founder of The Phoenix. *Cujus animae propitietur Deus*. 'He opened the doors of the Restoration Theatre' (Sir Edmund Gosse).

At 12 noon on 10th April Mr d'Arch Smith was 'at home' at his flat in St John's Wood, as host at a celebratory luncheon. The guests were Leslie Staples, Victor Hall (antiquarian bookseller), Cecil and Jean Woolf (the publishers of *The Galanty Show*), Devi Bruce (representing her mother, Sylvia Bruce), and myself. Mr and Mrs Woolf had brought with them advance copies of the 'special' edition of the book, which was limited to thirty copies, choicely bound, with decorative end-papers, additional plates, and a photo-facsimile of a letter from Summers to A.J.A. Symons, which I had found in the library of Princeton University, N.J. After the meal we drank a toast to the memory of Montague Summers, and it was a most happy occasion. Leslie, now eighty-four, was in splendid form, in spite of a recent and difficult spell in hospital, and was overjoyed to hold in his hands at last the long-awaited volume.

He died only three months later, on 21st July. His memorial service was held at Saint George the Martyr's, in The Borough: 'Little Dorrit's church'. On the outer page of the order of service were printed these words from Dickens's Christmas story, 'The Holly Tree Inn': 'He was a gentleman of spirit, and good looking, and held up his head when he walked, and had what you may call Fire about him.' A good description of our friend.

I think it was Colin Wilson who introduced me in 1963 to Geraldine Lady Strabolgi, the widow of the Labour peer, the first baron Strabolgi, formerly Lieutenant-Commander Kenworthy, RN, MP, of whom a large portrait in oils dominated the living room of her flat in Kensington. She was interested in a number of the younger writers of the day, whom I used sometimes to meet at her 'evenings'. It was there that I used to meet her friend and confidante, the Dowager Countess of Craven. Mary Silverthorne, who was sometimes at these gatherings, was always amused by Mina Craven's formula for making an early departure: "Well, must be gettin' back to Berkshire now."

Geraldine Strabolgi and Mina Craven were staunch Catholics; they had both suffered considerably from tensions and hostilities within their families. Among their close friends were Charles Richard Cammell and his wife Iona, with whom I spent, over a period of years, many pleasant evenings at their house, Number 100 Drayton Gardens, when we often dined at a splendid Greek restaurant in the Fulham Road. Their story is told in Charles's two autobiographies: *Heart of Scotland* and *Castles in the Air*. Charles Cammell, Old Etonian, and a fine poet of the traditional school – his *Collected Poems* were published as early as 1926 by Martin Secker – was a frequent contributor to the *Aylesford Review*; but he did not hesitate to make known to me his dislike of some of the more 'modern' verse that we were printing. Cammell's best prose work was his life of Charles Villiers, the first Duke of Buckingham, and of his poetry pride of place must be given to his long poem *The Triumph of Beauty*, and to his satire, written in heroic couplets, on vivisectors and vivisection. In Edinburgh, where they had lived for many years, Charles and Iona had known John Gray and André Raffalovich; later, in the southern kingdom, they knew Hilary Pepler and Montague Summers. In my estimation Charles Cammell was a noble man, a striking bearded figure, of lean height, with his stick, trews, and Tam-O'Shanter. I hope that his portrait is in the National Portrait Gallery of Scotland. It ought to be.

Geraldine Strabolgi and Mina Craven died while I was in Canada. They were survivals, lively survivals, from an earlier day. They would have fitted perfectly into the scenes and surroundings portrayed in the novels of Maurice Baring.

From 1967, when he came to Allington Castle to speak to an invited audience about the ideas put forward in his book *Europe: Faith and Plan*, I often saw Sir Oswald Mosley. I last saw him, six months before his death in 1981, at a reception given in a London hotel for the publication of his wife's biography of the Duchess of Windsor. I was saddened to see that for the first time since I had known him he was showing his age. He was seated at a table, deep in conversation with old friends from his earlier days in politics, and I felt that I ought not to disturb him. Lady Mosley noticed the situation, and thought otherwise, explaining the situation to his friends, since I was not able to stay long. Very kindly they moved aside, so as to allow me a few minutes of private conversation with him. I think he sensed that we would not meet again, for he was especially affectionate in his manner when I took my leave of him. I have only once had a similar experience, and that was at my last meeting, in 1940, with someone of very different outlook: Eric Gill.

Diana Mosley I still see from time to time, and her sister Mrs Jackson, who lives near Cheltenham. In recent years Lady Mosley has become a deservedly popular writer of elegant biographies and memoirs. The rare brilliance of her quarterly magazine of the 1950s, *The European*, is still remembered. The sight of her lively cursive script on an envelope always raises my spirits in anticipation of the interesting letter it will contain.

Two of my closest friends for twenty years were Frances Horovitz and Gabriel Wall, women of outstanding gifts, who died from cancer in their mid-forties, Frances in 1983, Gabriel in 1985.

Frances was forty-five when she died, and was well known as a poet, and also as a *BBC* poetry reader, and as a radio and television actress. Even her greatest admirers were astonished at the *réclame* she received immediately after her death. Since then her *Collected Poems* have been published; also a small book, *Frances Horovitz, Poet*, which contains memoirs of her by Jane Percival, Oswald Jones, and myself, and an appreciation of her poetry by Peter Levi. Frances is buried in the churchyard at Orcop, in Herefordshire, the parish where she spent the last year or so of her life, in the Welsh border-country that inspired many of her last poems.

Gabriel was a year older than Frances. She was the younger daughter of Barbara Wall – the novelist Barbara Lucas – whom I had known at Ditchling in the 1930s, when she had been for a time engaged to Mark Pepler. Later she married Bernard Wall, editor of *Colosseum* and *The Twentieth Century*, writer and Italian scholar. Gabriel had married, when she was still very young, the critic Bernard Bergonzi, lecturer in English at Warwick University. In the early 1970s, when her three children were of school age, Gabriel graduated at, successively, Leicester and Warwick universities, and became a highly successful teacher. Had she lived longer she would probably have made a name for herself as a writer. A little before her death she was experimenting with the writing of short stories, and was beginning to paint. Two short pieces that she wrote about her struggle with cancer have been privately printed.

Gabriel once said in a letter to me: 'My life seems to me one long adventure and voyage of self-discovery.' A Dominican friend of hers, who wrote to me after her death, said: 'Gabriel struck me as an immensely free person, who didn't mistake the structures of life for the purpose of living'. That sums her up well.

I must not omit to make some mention of the many agreeable and profitable hours that I have spent in the company of my Dominican friend Fr Bede Bailey, especially in the years when I spent some weeks each summer as locum tenens in the parish of Saint Thomas of Canterbury, Newport, Isle of Wight. Fr Bede, custodian of the Dominican provincial archives, was then located a mile or so up the road, as chaplain to the Dominican contemplative nuns at Carisbrooke. Since then he has removed, with the archives, to Edinburgh. Happily, he is an excellent correspondent. Because the area of his erudition coincides with some of my own spheres of special interest – not least the Catholic writers and artists of the *fin de siècle* – I profit much from his letters. Another erudite and entertaining correspondent is Brother Donald Halliday, whom I first met, in 1937, at Mount Olivet Monastery, Frensham, in the days of Brother Joseph Gard'ner. Brother Donald has succeeded the late Peter Anson as our leading scholar in the field of English post-Reformation monastic life. If only he could be persuaded to put pen to paper.

CHAPTER ELEVEN

A Willing Exile

In 1968 there was a new prior at Aylesford, and a new provincial superior. The new prior was Fr Berchmans Hearne, a capable administrator and a very pleasant *confrère* to live with. His principal achievement during his term of office was the transfer of the library from the room in which it had been set up to the Earl of Aylesford's former hall of state. The new provincial superior was Dr Kilian Lynch, who continued to live at The Friars.

During the summer it became known that the Pope (Paul VI: G.B. Montini) was about to issue an encyclical letter on the birth control question. This thorny subject had been withdrawn by the Pope from the agenda of the recent Second Vatican Council, so that the bishops had been unable to discuss it. In an address given on 23rd July, 1964 the Pope had said that the Church – by which he seems to have meant himself – was studying the birth control question, and that in the mean time 'we must say openly that up to now we have not sufficient reason to consider the rules laid down by Pius XII on this matter to be out of date and therefore not binding.' However, this statement did not seem to exclude the possibility that the accepted teaching could be revised or re-interpreted. In the same discourse the Pope had said that the Church would have to proclaim the law of God 'in the light of the scientific, social, and psychological truths which in these times have undergone new and very ample study and documentation.'

Writing in *The Tablet*, the premier English Catholic weekly, as late as 8th May, 1968, the Archbishop of Westminster, Cardinal Heenan, had spoken of the 'isolation' of the Pope from the bishops, and said that in the matter of birth control the ordinary teaching authority of the Church seemed to have lost its nerve. 'If, indeed,' he said, 'the old principles are to be adapted to the changed condition of our time, Catholics resent this long period of suspense.' This was plain speaking; the Cardinal could hardly have said more clearly that in his view a change in or modification of the old teaching was possible.

At the end of July the Pope's decision was made known. It was received by most educated English Catholics, and no doubt by many of the less well educated also, with incredulity and dismay; and it was the same in many other countries: not, perhaps, so much on account of the decision itself as because of the way it had been made. For everyone knew, from the press and radio, that all but four members of the commission which the Pope had set up to advise him had not only said that the standard teaching could be changed, but had recommended that it should be. The thirty-odd members of the commission included cardinals, bishops, priests, doctors, and fathers and mothers of families. The minority report, which concluded that no change was possible, was the work of four men, all of them priests of the Society of Jesus. It was this minority report that the Pope had chosen to accept.

On 4th August, a Saturday, I had to go to Sheerness, to hear confessions in the evening and celebrate two of the parish Masses on Sunday morning. At each Mass I was expected to preach; and the congregations would be expecting to hear from the pulpit some- thing about the Pope's decision. It would not be right, I thought, to dodge the issue by preaching on the Gospel of the Sunday. And yet, it would surely be improper to criticize, or attempt to 'water down', a papal document from someone else's pulpit? Happily, the parish priest solved the problem for me. It would be best, he thought, – and he had no inkling of what was in my mind – if the people were simply told that the encyclical would be explained to them in a pastoral letter from the bishop of the diocese which would be read to them on the Sunday following.

On the next day, Monday 6th August, this letter to the editor appeared in *The Times*.

Sir, The publication of the encyclical letter 'Humanae vitae' shows, if nothing else, that the Orthodox and other Eastern Churches are fully justified in their mistrust of the papal office as it has developed over the centuries since the Great Schism. The 'primacy of love' known to the early, undivided Church has long since been replaced by the 'Roman', and, indeed, Italian monarchic primacy of jurisdiction, conceived in an autocratic and absolutist sense. Here is the problem, and it is to the East that we must look for its solution.

The present Pope a few years ago made a significant pilgrimage to the tomb of San Celestino. If he would now resign his see, as did St Celestine, and make it possible for one of the Oriental patriarchs to succeed him, the Latin Church might yet be saved from ignominious dissolution.

In the mean time, until we are censured for doing so, many of us who have pastoral responsibilities of one kind or another will continue to bear in mind the maxim: '*Impossibili nemo tenetur*'.

Yours etc.,

Brocard Sewell

Looked at today this letter seems to me a compound of sound sense, Corvine humour, and exasperation. I had not really expected that *The Times* would print it. For a simple friar to call for the Pope's resignation was certainly a bit strong. All the same, a cat may look at a king, as the saying has it. Someone might not unreasonably have asked who I thought I was?, but no one did. A new Savonarola, perhaps? But that was far from being so. I had no wish to be unfrocked, excommunicated, or imprisoned in the Castle of Saint Angelo. But I do believe today, nearly a quarter of a century later, that the pontificate of Paul VI was, on several counts, and not just because of *Humanae vitae*, one of the most disastrous in history.

The element of Corvine humour in my letter to *The Times* was not detected by authority, nor would it have been appreciated if it had. Some readers did not understand that the Oriental patriarchs mentioned were not Orthodox bishops, but Eastern-rite Catholics, in communion with Rome. I should have expressed myself more clearly on that point.

The next morning the Prior, Fr Hearne, spoke to me about the letter, which he had not seen on the previous day, and said that he was grieved that I had not consulted him before sending it. This I understood, and felt sorry about. But if I had shown him the letter it could not have been sent, because he would have put me under obedience not to send it. Fr Hearne had always been very kind to me, and I certainly had not wanted to involve him in any trouble on my account. But I felt that some such public statement of dissent from within the ranks of the clergy was required, in order to help all those lay people who were burdened in conscience over the birth control question. I did not think that I would be the only priest publicly to dissent; but there was no means of knowing whether dissenters would be many or few. And it was easier for me to express dissent than it was for many others. As a member of the regular (that is, monastic) clergy I was not dependent on any bishop for my livelihood, and so had little to lose.

On the Wednesday morning my higher superior, Dr Kilian Lynch, brought to my room a letter he had received from the Latin-Rite Bishop of Southwark saying that I was no longer *persona grata* in his diocese, and that he must require of me a recantation. This I said I was unable to make, so I was told by Dr Lynch to settle up all my affairs quickly, and be ready to leave the house in two days' time. He would inform me of my place of banishment later. I surmised that it was likely to be our college at Aberystwyth.

At this point it seemed to me sensible to request a month's leave of absence, so that I might have time to consider my position. This was agreed to. The next day I received a letter from the Vicar General of the diocese telling me that I was suspended from preaching and hearing confessions within the diocese, though not from saying Mass. Seven other priests of the diocese, six secular priests and one canon regular, were likewise suspended. All these had voiced their dissent from the pulpit on the previous Sunday.

A month later the bishop was obliged to withdraw all the suspensions. The best canon lawyer in the country had shown him conclusively that in conferring these sanctions he had acted *ultra vires*. The encyclical letter *Humanae vitae*, like other encyclical letters, was not in the most solemn category of papal pronouncements, such as are held to be, in technical language, 'infallible'. Neither the bishop nor Dr Lynch informed me that the suspensions had been lifted; I read of it in *The Times*. Since I had by then left the diocese, the bishop very likely felt that it was not his responsibility to inform me.

Kilian Lynch, an American citizen of Irish origin, was a hard man, and would never admit to having made a mistake, though occasionally he would withdraw silently from a position that he found had become untenable. Yet there was, of course, another side to him. In some ways he was a genuinely humble man; or, as he would have said in his strange accent, a blend of Dublin and the Bronx, "umble'. When he retired as Prior General he could have had a Red Hat had he so wished, in the days of Papa Pacelli (Pius XII), whom he knew well. Or a mitre. His name was once submitted to the Holy See by the chapter of the diocese for the vacant bishopric of Ferns, in Ireland, and there are said to have been other such nominations. But nothing came of them, in part because he was not interested. He would have agreed with Fr Bede Jarrett, the great Dominican, that religious in high positions of authority cannot have friends within their Order. Dr Lynch remained, even after his retirement, a lonely man, I think, even though he had mellowed. Certainly he was a great Carmelite, and one of the great priors general. He deserves a biography, but who could write it? He left no personal correspondence, and no personal diaries. He lived for the Order, and had no other interests.

I next applied for, and was granted, a year's leave of absence, and went to stay with my old friends Helen and Wilfrid Davies and their family at Capel-y- ffin. The domestic chapel set up by Eric Gill in the former monastery was still in use, and the Bishop of Menevia, a more sensible man than his brother at Southwark, made no difficulty over licensing me to celebrate Mass, preach, and hear confessions in his diocese. (Helen Davies, my hostess for the next year or so, was the eldest grand-daughter of both Hilary Pepler and Eric Gill.)

In the previous autumn a London publisher had commissioned me to write a book on the current crisis in the church. The result was *The Vatican Oracle*, on which I had put in a lot of hard work, and long hours of research in the British Museum Reading Room and at Saint Deiniol's Library at Hawarden, near Chester. The book was published in 1970, and was a nicely produced volume, with a striking dust-jacket. It did not receive many reviews. Perhaps the timing of its publication was not right, a plethora of books to do with 'Vatican Two' having already been published. Such reviews as it did receive were favourable, the most appreciative being that by Canon F.H. Drinkwater in *The Tablet*. Surprisingly, the book sold only a few hundred copies, and was promptly – too promptly, perhaps? – remaindered. I felt sorry for the publisher, but could not help wondering if he had promoted the book as effectively as he might have done. Perhaps part of the trouble was the book's title, *The Vatican Oracle*, with its echoes of Montalembert's famous *L'Idole du Vatican*. This seemed a good idea at the time; but I fancy it may have contributed to the book's failure. For one thing, it gave no clue whatever to what the book was about; some people may even have thought that it was a novel. However, when I take it down from my shelves, as I occasionally do, – it is quite a useful work of reference in some respects – I find it interesting and readable. It contains much information about the Church's formulations in the field of sexual morality which it would not be easy to find elsewhere.

Before I left Aylesford Priory a notice was sent to all subscribers to the *Aylesford Review* to tell them that publication of the magazine was suspended. In the event it was never resumed. One of the subscribers was the Reverend R.J. McSween, chairman of the department of English at Saint Francis Xavier University in Antigonish, Nova Scotia. One day early in 1969 I received in my Welsh retreat a letter from Fr McSween asking me if I would like to come to Antigonish to teach some seminar courses on the Pre-Raphaelites and the *fin-de-siècle* writers of the 1890s; and also to edit and help launch a new magazine that the University was sponsoring. This seemed providential, and was an exciting prospect. I had no special knowledge of the Pre-Raphaelites, but I knew that I was regarded – for a writer in the *Times Literary Supplement* had said so – as an authority on the aesthetes and decadents among the writers of the 1890s. And I certainly had had some experience of editing magazines. I thus found myself, with the approval of my superiors, a willing exile. (*A Willing Exile*: this is the title of a novel by the minor 1890s writer André Raffalovich.)

On 25th August, 1969 I left Heathrow airport on an Air Canada flight to Halifax, Nova Scotia, a six hour journey. We touched down at 4.30 p.m, Eastern Standard Time; in England it would still have been only about 10.30 a.m. As we came off the plane we stepped into a dry, crackling heat of about ninety degrees Fahrenheit. I was met by Fr McSween, who had brought with him the Dean of Arts from the University, Fr Malcolm MacDonnell.

I liked Canada from the moment I stepped off the aircraft, the Canadians too. The long winters were to make me wonder, sometimes, such is their length and savagery; but when the winter did at last come to an end one soon recovered from such feelings. There is a saying in Canada that either you are preparing for winter, or it is winter, or you are getting over winter. That is very much how it is.

The name Antigonish is a North American Indian name. It is pronounced with the accent on the final syllable. This little town is on Canada's eastern seaboard, and faces towards Prince Edward Island, which is clearly visible from Antigonish harbour. Main Street, Antigonish's principal thoroughfare, was originally called Joe's Snake Trail; it is now the shopping centre, with the post office, cinema, banks, stores (shops), and the Wandlyn Motel. A few of the public buildings are of stone or brick; most of the stores, and nearly all the houses, are of wood, painted white, as is the principal Anglican church, quite a large building, with a steeple. A little beyond it is the residence of the Catholic bishop, a large but unpretentious wooden house, with a small turret that lends it dignity. The town spreads out to the north, with tree-lined streets – the trees are mostly maples – and whitewashed wooden 'frame' houses of the former colonial pattern.

The inhabitants of Antigonish are largely of Scots descent, the descendants of immigrants from the Highland 'clearances', and are most of them Catholics. The façades of many of the shops bear such names as Gillis, Monro, McLean, Macdonald, Frazer, and so on. The topography of this part of Nova Scotia is very much like that of the Lowlands of Scotland. Gaelic is still spoken by some of the older people, and is taught in the University. The tombstones of early settlers in the churchyards at Glen Bard and Arisaig, a few miles from Antigonish, have Gaelic inscriptions. In Antigonish the popu- lation of between four and five thousand is still mainly Catholic. The biggest church in Antigonish is Saint Ninian's Cathedral, now about a hundred years old. It is quite an impressive stone building, faintly Classical in style, with interior decoration that shows an Italian influence. Over the central portal the Irish labourers who built it have mischievously carved a shamrock where there ought to be a thistle. On the hilltop overlooking the cathedral is the university campus. There are between two and three thousand students. The campus is well laid out, with lawns and trees. Most of the buildings are of brick. There is a big university church, a football stadium, a sports centre, and the Angus L. Macdonald Library (named after a benefactor).

Saint Francis Xavier University, known to its alumni as Saint F.-X., was founded in 1853 by Bishop Hamilton MacDonald, not in Antigonish, but in Arichat, a few miles away. Two years later it was transferred to Antigonish, and in 1866 it received its charter from the Provincial Legislature. The University is the product of the dedication and sacrifice of the Catholic people and clergy of the area. Today it is funded by Government grant, and is open to all, irrespective of religious denomination. The students are mostly Nova Scotians, but some of them come from other parts of Canada, and from the United States and other countries.

Earlier in the present century the English writer and radio and television personality Gilbert Harding taught for a time in the English faculty at Saint F.-X. He is still remembered, but not altogether favourably. He did not stay long. In his biography, *Along My Line*, the four and a half pages that he allots to his sojourn in Nova Scotia are not over complimentary. The book was published in 1953, and he says that Antigonish, 'which is now a large and flourishing university, was in those days finding its feet with some difficulty as a place of learning.' He found the students very backward, some of them scarcely literate. He complains of their bad manners, and says that he found it difficult to teach them anything at all. Things have much improved since then.

In 1969 there were about a hundred and forty teachers at Saint F.-X., of whom forty or so were priests. Among the hundred and forty there were less than half a dozen women. Soon after I arrived there was a clergy conference to discuss 'Traditional and New Ideas on the nature and purpose of a Catholic University'. None of the speakers was able to define what was meant by the term 'Catholic University'. In fact, it was questioned whether today there could be such a thing, except perhaps in the limited sense of a university that is in some way approved or supported by the Church.

The Chancellor of Saint Francis Xavier University is the Bishop of Antigonish. This has always been so. Until very recently the President also was a priest; but no longer. The priests teaching in the University shared a common refectory in Morrison Hall, a clergy residence where I had my quarters. This meant that the

priests lived rather apart from their lay *confrères*, men and women
whom they rarely met at meals. Not a good arrangement, I think.
The bishop, Dr Power, a friendly and approachable man, would
quite often drop in for the evening meal, and obviously enjoyed his
priests' company. An important event each year was the Saint
Andrew's Night dinner, on 30th November, when a haggis,
specially flown in from Scotland, was borne into the refectory by
the chef, preceded by a kilted piper. To the music of the pipes they
marched solemnly around the refectory, and then the President of
the University made the customary address to the haggis in Gaelic.
In the summer the town or city of Antigonish was thronged for the
annual Highland Games, which are as spectacular as those held at
Braemar.

In the autumn of 1969 the pride of the University was the
recently opened new Academic Centre, officially named, after a
former President, Nicholson Hall. This was an impressive tower-
block building of the steel, glass, and concrete kind, containing lecture rooms, seminar rooms, auditoria, and spacious faculty
offices. On the top floor was a large and comfortable faculty lounge,
where the teachers met for their mid-morning coffee. Nicholson
Hall was, I think, the only building on the campus with air-
conditioning: a great blessing in the scorching Canadian summer —
as long as it was functioning properly.

From the start I enjoyed teaching Canadian students. Certainly
most of them were academically rather behind British students of
the same age. As regards the English language, they were handicapped (but so are British students now, one understands) by
lack of knowledge of grammar, so that some found it difficult to
construct a really coherent and cohering sentence; and with few
was spelling their strong point. But they were most of them, the
great majority, willing and anxious to learn. I had two seminar
classes, each meeting twice a week. In one group there were twelve
students, in the other twenty. Young men were outnumbered by
girls; and in my second class there were three nuns. These seminar
courses on the Pre-Raphaelites and the Aesthetes and Decadents
of the 1890s were an 'extra' on the syllabus; so every student
attending them was there of his or her own free choice. It was
chiefly the name Oscar Wilde that had attracted them.

A few had been attracted by Baron Corvo; Harry Luke's dramatized version of Corvo's *Hadrian the Seventh* had recently been presented in Toronto. This had been seen by one of my students, Michael Higgins, who while at Saint F.-X. wrote a play about Corvo for radio. It was not a bad effort, and I was disappointed when it failed to get accepted by the CBC. After graduating at Saint F.-X. Michael Higgins went on to gain a doctorate from the University of Toronto, and today he teaches at the University of Saint Jerome's College, part of the University of Waterloo, Ontario, but with its own independent university status.

Our seminars were conducted with the minimum of formality. Sometimes we met in one of the smaller lecture rooms, but mostly we used one of the seminar rooms in Nicholson Hall, where there were reasonably comfortable chairs, and an upholstered bench which ran along one side of the room. One young couple, Susan Hay and Terry Lenihan, always sat together on this bench, holding hands, usually with their eyes shut. They gave the impression of being concerned with other things than William Morris, the Rossettis, Burne-Jones, Ernest Dowson, and John Gray; but their assignments were always well done, and their examination results good. They came from Bathurst, in New Brunswick, where they had been friends since childhood. After they left the University they married. Since then they have done well, Susan as a very success-ful teacher of English and Drama, Terry in the Law. On a sub-sequent visit to Canada I witnessed his admission to the Canadian Bar, at Fredericton, in a simple ceremony conducted in Latin.

One evening in early February 1970 three of my girl students arrived very late. After apologising, they handed me a large card-board box, wrapped in decorative paper, and told me to open it. Inside was a very pretty one-year- old ginger cat. Its name, they said, was BEARDSLEY. This was intended as a Saint Valentine's Day present, given a little in advance as we would not be meeting on that day. This pleasing gesture had been inspired, it appeared, by some remarks I had made at a previous class about George Arthur Rose's little cat, Flavio, in *Hadrian the Seventh*.

As in England and on the Continent of Europe, so in Canada this was a time of students' 'stirs' in the universities. In April 1971 the burning question of the day at Saint F.-X. was what was called 'Open Housing'. The women students, apart from a few who lived with their families in the town, or shared flats in the town with other girls, were housed in Saint Bernard's College, an institution run by nuns, where the régime was thought by the students to be restrictive. Most of the students, both men and women, wanted this state of things changed, and also there was a general demand that the present men's residences should be made open to both sexes. This demand the university authorities were unwilling to accept. There was strong resistance to it from the clergy, partly because it was feared that the introduction of 'open housing' would cause parents not to send their sons and daughters to the University.

A campaign of 'civil disobedience' was begun by the students, in protest, and a number of offences were committed: male and female students being found in each others' quarters after hours; and so on. Two hundred and six offenders, mostly men, were detected by the campus police. Three men, who were supposed to be ring-leaders, were brought before the University Disciplinary Committee, convicted, and sentenced. Many people thought that the offences alleged against them, or at least some of them, had not been sufficiently proven, and a very tense atmosphere began to make itself felt.

At 3 a.m. on the morning of 5th April a petrol bomb was thrown into the basement of Morrison Hall. A number of priests, myself among them, lived in this building, one of them being confined to his bed with advanced arterio-sclerosis. Fortunately, the fire brigade arrived within a few minutes, and the blaze was quickly put out. This was an isolated incident; the perpetrator was never discovered.

The next day a students' strike was declared, with a boycott of classes. Since the previous week some of the students had been on hunger strike. Most of the teachers showed little sympathy with them; at a meeting held to discuss the situation three members of the Faculty urged the advisability of securing for them medical advice and supervision; but on the whole this proposal was not well received.

In the meantime the University had obtained from the High Court of Nova Scotia an injunction restraining anyone from attempting to prevent access to classes; but there was no trouble of that kind. In fact, the students' leaders discouraged the use of violence, and the pickets outside Nicholson Hall were well behaved.

On 8th April, Holy Thursday, the University Senate met to consider the appeals of the three students who had been disciplined. Two of them had their fines remitted, and were given permission to receive their degrees *in absentia*. The third man, who had been expelled, was now allowed to do his final year at the University, but 'on probation'. He alone of the three was not satisfied. He was something of a demagogue, and when the students returned after the Easter break he persuaded them to resume the strike. At that point, on the Tuesday in Easter week, the authorities decided to close the University on account of the impossibility of holding classes in the atmosphere prevailing, with an increasing possibility of acts of violence.

Eventually the agitation died down, and a year or so later the University authorities capitulated over the Open Housing issue, and there was very little complaint or protest from any quarter.

My teaching schedule was purposely kept light so that I might give as much time as possible to the production of the new magazine. All the same, I had to do a good deal of study and research, especially in the matter of the Pre- Raphaelites. As far as English Literature was concerned the Angus L. Macdonald Library was only moderately good, in a patchy kind of way. It has improved in that respect since I was there, and from the students' point of view it has now been made more comfortable by the addition of a well-planned extension. I found, though, that the library's administration was generous in obtaining such new books as teachers might request.

In the autumn of '69 I was not the only recruit from Britain to the department of English at Saint F.-X. There was also a young Scots couple, Angus and Barbara Somerville, and a couple of mixed nationality, Derek and Grazia Wood, all of whom proved to be good friends and colleagues. The chairman of the department, Fr McSween, was a very fine teacher, much liked and admired by his students, and was a specialist on the life and work of Ezra Pound. It was a matter for surprise when one learned that so 'European' a man had never left the shores of Nova Scotia. 'Rod' McSween was a big, genial man, a great golfer, and the best of company. I felt, when I learned of his death in September 1990, that perhaps he had not fully realized all his potentialities in life; but on reflection I think he may well have achieved all that he wanted to achieve. And surely that is enough? Another good *confrère* in the department of English was Dr John L. MacPherson, who was a knight of the highest grade in the Sovereign and Military Order of Saint John of Jerusalem – the Knights of Malta: that is to say, he was, and is, a religious in solemn vows.

The magazine that I was to edit was to be called *The Antigonish Review*. The first number appeared, to some acclaim, in the spring of 1970. It was of the same format as the *Aylesford Review*, but had more pages: one hundred and thirty, no less, as against sixty or seventy. It was printed by offset-litho at the press of the local newspaper, and was a dignified, serious-looking production. I had been invited to Antigonish for one year, and had then been invited to remain for a second year. By the end of that time Fr McSween felt ready to take over the editorship himself, and I felt that my mission had been completed, and that it was time for me to return home. I have revisited Antigonish three times since then, the latest, but I hope not the last, in 1988.

It was at Antigonish that I first met Devendra Varma, professor of English at Dalhousie University, in Halifax, N.S., who came specially to see me in my quality of biographer of Montague Summers. Dr Varma is the doyen of scholars in the field of the Gothic Novel, and is Summers's successor in that rôle. For several years he has been one of the most appreciated contributors to our 'Aylesford' literary symposia, held each spring, formerly at Spode House, now at Wistaston Hall, in Crewe.

I was surprised and pleased when I was invited by Fr Paul Hoban, then provincial of the Canadian-American province of our Order, to return to Canada in the autumn of 1973, to teach English at Mount Carmel College, Niagara Falls, Ontario. The college, which dates back to 1827, is built on an escarpment only half a mile from the Falls. At first it had been a hospice and retreat centre, then a seminary for training the Order's future priests. In 1973 it was a combined high school and junior seminary for aspirants to membership of the Order. This proved an uneasy combination; the day for enterprises of that kind was really over. Still, it was a worthwhile attempt. Today Mount Carmel is again a retreat house and conference centre.

The handsome building, of stone and brick, is recognizably conventual, with Gothic and Romanesque features, and a small cloister. Standing in a setting of lawns and trees, its red roof makes a nice contrast in aerial photographs on fine days with the green grass and blue sky, and the blue of the Niagara river, which flows just below the escarpment.

In 1973 there were about eighty boys in the school, aged from about twelve to seventeen, most of them American. The community was made up of ten priests and three or four laybrothers. Most of the priests taught in the school; one of them was also the parish priest of the church of Our Lady of Peace, which stands within the grounds of the college. It is the oldest Catholic church in the Niagara Peninsula, quite a pleasing building, with a small steeple. The community was very observant: my diary for June 1973 says: 'I have never lived in a more harmonious community . . . All the priests here are dedicated teachers; given the disposition of the North American teenage boy this is something to marvel at.'

Actually, the average North American boy is a thoroughly like-able person; but he usually has a strong disinclination to learn anything at all. In all, I spent three years at Mount Carmel, and have only good memories of them. These include my making of Christmas puddings, from a recipe sent to me by Frances Horovitz – Christmas puddings seem to be unknown in Canada – and teaching the history of the Order, and of other religious orders, to our novices, who were living next door in a building known as Avila Hall.

I have always loved military and ecclesiastical ceremonial and spectacle. In the summer of 1975 there were two rather grand centenary celebrations in Britain in which I had some part. The first was my own brainchild: a celebration of the eighth centenary of the foundation of Llanthony Priory, a house of Augustinian Canons, in the vale of Ewyas, four miles below Fr Ignatius of Llanthony's nineteenth century monastery at Capel-y-ffin. The anniversary celebration was arranged by a joint Anglican-Roman Catholic committee, and took the form of a Solemn Evensong in the roofless ruin of the huge priory church, which Abbot Sir David Oswald Hunter-Blair always said was the most beautiful monastic ruin in Wales. It was a perfect day for the occasion. The Bishop of Monmouth presided, the Abbot of Bodmin (Dom Charles White), vested in cope and mitre, was the celebrant, and the Prior of Bodmin (Dom Ambrose Whitehead) preached a very fine sermon,

in all respects apposite to the occasion. The singing was led by
two united choirs, and the hymns were accompanied by the
Abergavenny Silver Band. A congregation of some five hundred
people had made it way to this, even today, quite remote spot.
A high point in the service was the singing of the Latin hymn
'Magne Pater Augustine' which had not been heard there since the
dissolution of the monastery in 1538.

The centenary of the death of Robert Stephen Hawker (+ 15th
August 1875) was observed at Morwenstow and also at Plymouth,
the place where he was born and died. The present Vicar of
Morwenstow had kindly invited me to read the Second Lesson at
the commemorative Sunday morning Mattins. In the sanctuary of
the Saxon church I was seated in the sedilia, beside the bishops
of Saint Germans (Richard Rutt, later Bishop of Leicester) and
Grantham (Peter Hawker, a collateral descendant of the poet). This
is the only time in my life when I have been publicly placed on a
par with bishops. (Dom Edward Kelly and myself encountered
when we were students, in the lanes of Hertfordshire, an *episcopus
vagans* who kindly offered to consecrate us both as bishops.
Unfortunately, there was a stipulation that we were unable to meet
– a stole fee of £50 each.) At a priedieu on the other side of
the chancel, was Dr Michael Ramsey, the retired Archbishop of
Canterbury, who preached a beautiful commemorative sermon, in
which he spoke of Hawker as "a beyond man in a beyond place".

After the service I looked among the congregation for Henry
Williamson, whose home was only a few miles away; but he was not
there. Already, though I did not know it, his memory was becoming
unreliable; but I did encounter Ronald Duncan, poet and play-
wright, who lived in Welcombe, the next parish, just over the
Devon border, which Hawker had administered, in addition to
Morwenstow. I was fortunate enough to have been asked to lunch at
the house where Dr Ramsey was staying, and was able to have a
good conversation with him as we drank our pre-lunch sherry. He
was surely unique; we shall not see his like again. His former press
secretary, Michael De-la-Noy, has captured him well in his memoir,
Michael Ramsey: A Portrait.

In the autumn of 1975 I returned to Canada; but in the summer
of 1977 I was back in England for a few weeks. On 13th August,
when I was staying with my god-daughter, Jennifer Bell, at

Jaywick Sands, in Essex, the death of Henry Williamson was announced on the radio and television news. It was entirely unexpected by me, and came as a shock. Henry had always been a very fit man. He had kept himself so by the manual work that he did on his land at Ox's Cross, near Georgeham, in Devon. This offset the effects of his long, sedentary writing hours. A year or two before his eightieth birthday, though, – he had been born in 1895 – his health very gradually began to give way. The post-war years had been difficult for him; he had been working against time, often under discouraging conditions, and almost without domestic help, to complete his huge masterpiece, the fifteen-volume novel sequence, *A Chronicle of Ancient Sunlight*. He was still to some extent under a cloud because of his pre-war and wartime 'deviationist' politics.

So his tired brain had taken its own escape route from the trials and tribulations of life. Although his memory was to some extent affected, his recollection of those battle scenes of the Somme and Paschendaele in which he had taken part, and of which he had written the truest accounts in English literature, remained as clear as ever. For the time being, until his family should be able to care for him themselves, he was looked after by the Alexian Hospitaller Brothers at Twyford Abbey, in north-west London, which is where I last saw him. Later, one of the Brothers told me that although he was sometimes confused as to time and place, Henry was physically in relatively good health for his age. He was eighty-one. His death came quickly, and was peaceful. He was conscious, and knew what was happening. He was well prepared.

Henry's funeral was at Georgeham. The ancient parish church, so often mentioned in his tales of Devon life, was filled by a congregation of about two hundred people, mostly his family, neighbours, and friends. There was little or no official representation; that came later, at the memorial service in London. Henry's grave is close to the hedge on the west side of the churchyard, a few yards from the church tower. During the commital a swarm of bees hovered uncomfortably near the grave and the officiating clergy. That would have amused him; it seemed appropriate.

After the funeral, guests were welcomed by the family in the house at Ox's Cross that Henry had recently built in his famous Field, but had never lived in. With me were Frances Horovitz and another great friend of Henry's, his former secretary, Kerstin Hegarty. Also his faithful driver and companion on many expeditions, Oswald Jones. Only six years later, alas, and Frances had joined Henry in the ancient sunlight of eternity. The weather on the day of Henry's funeral was fine; after the service most of the guests assembled at Ox's Cross, where they drank tea and talked of Henry as they stood in the open air and sunshine outside the house, which would have been too small to contain them all. In the church and at the graveside there had been tears; but now there was a feeling of happiness. Happiness for Henry that the sufferings and anxieties of life were over for him, not least the trials of old age; happiness among his friends as they talked of him to one another.

CHAPTER TWELVE

Envoi

O all-pervading Spirit! Sacred beam!
Parent of life and light! Eternal Power!
Grant me through obvious clouds one transient gleam
Of thy bright essence in my dying hour!

William Beckford: 'A Prayer': lines written at Fonthill Abbey

Enjoying humbly the most precious gift of Heaven to man – Hope!

William Beckford: *Vathek*

As Sir Positive At-All, a sententious knight in Thomas Shadwell's splendid comedy *The Sullen Lovers*, observes: 'Betwixt you and I, let me tell you, we are all mortal.' To have reached and passed three score years and ten is still an awesome thing. Our family tends to be long-lived. Of the Victorians, for example, James Edwards Sewell, Warden of New College, Oxford, from 1860 to 1903, lived to be ninety-three; his sister Elizabeth Missing Sewell, the novelist and educationalist, reached ninety-one. In the next generation my grandfather Arthur Sewell lived to within a few days of his one hundred and fifth birthday. My father, however, died at seventy-two; but only, I think, because he had continued teaching at a time when he should have been under medical care. I do not rate my own possibilities of longevity very high; though, as the butler, so admirably played by the late Stanley Holloway, in Bernard Shaw's comedy says: 'You never can tell.' In the ordinary course of events, though, it can hardly be very long now before the Present latches its postern behind my tremulous stay. So the dominical injunction 'Watch, therefore, for ye know not the day nor the hour,' rings in my mind. And I remember the prayer of Saint Thomas More, written in

161

the Tower of London: 'Give me thy grace, good Lord, to have ever afore mine eye my death that is ever at hand.' In a letter which he wrote to Hilary Pepler in August 1932 Fr Vincent McNabb said: '. . . at sixty-five one must be bustling to depart. Only the most urgent things can be seen to.' (He lived to be seventy-three.) So now I ask what still remains urgent to me?

First, there is the matter of religion. How and where do I stand? My position today is certainly rather different from what it was when I became a Catholic in 1930. At school I went through a brief phase of unbelief; today I see that there are stronger grounds for unbelief than I realized at the age of fourteen; but I still reject unbelief. As Owen Chadwick has said in an essay on Newman: 'Only a corrupt mind could believe that all the religious experience reported by the human race is nothing but a buzzing in the ears.' Yet at the same time one must recognize that, as Newman puts it in *Parochial and Plain Sermons* (1.221) 'Religious light is intellectual darkness. We see now through a glass darkly.' Arthur Machen, believer and churchman, liked to repeat the medieval tag: *Omnia exeunt in mysterium.*

However, I take my stand on John Locke's affirmation, in the *Essay Concerning Human Understanding*: 'Man knows by an intuitive certainty that bare nothing can no more produce any real being than it can be equal to two right angles.' In other words: 'Nothing can come from nothing. Think again.' From that it is only a short step to Aristotle's and Aquinas's unmoved mover: *Nihil movetur nisi ab alio movetur*, and all that follows from that principle.

> Meanwhile, I know where difficulties lie
> I could not, cannot solve, nor ever shall,
> so give up hope accordingly to solve . . .

Does this mean, then, that one must lapse into scepticism or agnosticism?

> Calm and complete, determinately fixed
> Today, tomorrow, and for ever, pray?
> You'll guarantee me that? Not so, I think!
> In no wise! all we've gained is, that belief,

As unbelief before, shakes us by fits,
Confounds us like its predecessor. Where's the gain?
Browning, *Bishop Blougram's Apology*)

From God to the Church is quite a step; but it is a logical
step. The Church on earth is made up of sinful human beings –
redeemed humanity is not a sinless humanity – so she does not
always appear as immediately attractive. I saw that less clearly
sixty or so years ago, when I identified the 'true' church with
ultramontane Roman Catholicism. When, much later, I had to
make a serious study of church history, I saw that this would not
quite do; but I still believe that the right notion of church order
is that of a visible society, with a ministry of bishops, priests,
and deacons, standing in the apostolic succession, affirming the
historic creeds, and administering the sacraments. And I believe
that the bishops of the church, and their flocks, should be in
communion with the chief bishop, the bishop of Rome, who inherits
the primacy of blessed Peter in the apostolic college.

Which brings me to my membership of the Carmelite Order.
The first Carmelites were hermits, living on Mount Carmel in the
Holy Land. When the Turks conquered the Latin Kingdom of
Jerusalem the hermits migrated to Europe, in or about the year
1242. Their Rule was then mitigated, in accordance with their
changed living conditions, and they were re-formed as an order of
mendicant friars. The central injunction of the Rule written for
them by Saint Albert of Vercelli, Latin patriarch of Jerusalem, was
left unchanged: 'Each one of you is to remain in his own cell, or
near it, by day and by night, watchful in prayer, and meditating on
the law of the Lord, unless some other duty prevents.' Some readers
of this book may feel like asking to what extent I have observed
this injunction? The saving clause in this precept is: 'unless some
other duty prevents.' This admits of, and even requires, a fairly
wide interpretation; but the question always is: how wide?

At a time of life when, by the benevolent disposition of my
superiors, I am able to spend as much, if not more, time in my cell
as outside it, I am conscious that it behoves me to cultivate a new
vigilance and self-discipline in the way I spend my time there.
Would three hours a day be too much to give to the study of the
Scriptures, the Fathers of the undivided Church, and the great

scholastic divines, not forgetting contemporary theologians of merit? I would think not. Yet can one hope to achieve such an ideal? I doubt it.

Towards the end of one's life one can hardly help asking, though the question is an uncomfortable one, what one has achieved in the time one has been given? Other uncomfortable questions arise. Could one perhaps have chosen the wrong vocations in life? And is it possible that one has mishandled the calling finally settled on? In his diary for 27th May, 1946 William Coldstream wrote: 'I feel still the doubts as to my suitability to being a professional painter – the same doubts that I first remember torturing me – if that's not too strong a word – when I was twenty-two. I ought to have become a doctor.' (From 'William Coldstream's Notebooks', selected by Caroline Cuthbert, in Lawrence Gowing and David Sylvester's *The Paintings of William Coldstream 1908-1987*: London, 1990.) He may have thought so, but can one imagine him as anything *but* a painter?

As to the matter of human achievement, perhaps we can take comfort from the words of Mr Bankes in *To the Lighthouse*: 'But the number of men who make a definite contribution to anything whatsoever is very small.' Perhaps my own modest contribution has been to literature, in the form of biographies or memoirs of some men and women of merit who have been overlooked or forgotten: Philip Thomas Howard, seventeenth-century Dominican and cardinal; John Gray, priest and poet; Olive Custance and Frances Horovitz, poets; Cecil Chesterton, political journalist and pamphleteer; Montague Summers, scholar and divine; Hilary Pepler, private press printer; Reginald Joseph Gard'ner, actor, impresario, and religious founder.

In conclusion I offer to my readers these words of the sage G.I. Gurdjieff: 'God and all his holy angels keep us from doing evil by helping us always and everywhere to remember our Selves.'

Index

Index

IN THE DORIAN MODE: A Life of John Gray: 1866–1934
Brocard Sewell
Under the patronage of Oscar Wilde, John Gray, a young civil servant from a working class background, became known as a poet and critic. But in 1898 he left London, was ordained in 1901, and spent the rest of his life in Edinburgh. Here he again began to write and publish, both poetry and prose, his new work being markedly 'modern' in manner. John Gray, who had once been rumoured to be the prototype of Oscar Wilde's fictional Dorian Gray, died in 1934. Twenty-two of Gray's poems are here reprinted and a chapter is devoted to his short novel *Park: A Fantastic Story.*
'Brocard Sewell's brilliant biography' A.N. Wilson, *The Literary Review*
'A most fascinating story sympathetically told' Fiona MacCarthy, *The Times*
Illustrated. 272 pp. Cased. £18.00

LIKE THE BLACK SWANS: Some People and Themes
Brocard Sewell. With an Introduction by **Colin Wilson**
Brocard Sewell's varied career is reflected in this selection from his occasional papers. *Like Black Swans* contains eleven biographical essays and concludes with two pieces on monastic life today and Catholic spirituality.
'Fr Brocard, himself a black swan, should clearly complete the dozen . . . he concludes with two pieces marked by his large comprehension, his respect for tradition and his contemporary awareness. *Like Black Swans* is finely produced, printed and illustrated, and it is introduced by Colin Wilson, an appropriate choice for those rare birds that are a type of outsider. Fr Brocard gives such pleasure that he arouses the hope that he will describe others of the species.'
The Tablet
Illustrated. 256 pp. Cased. Limited edition of 500 signed copies. £18.00

HENRY WILLIAMSON, The Man, The Writings: A Symposium of Essays
Edited by **Brocard Sewell** with an Introduction by **Ronald Duncan** and an Address by **Ted Hughes**
'An excellent and comprehensive guide to Williamson's books, and a mine of information.' *Literary Review*
'Fourteen contributors combine here to re-establish a gifted writer. His country books (*Tarka* especially) derive from Richard Jefferies: in them he surpasses his inspirer.' *Now!*
'Diana Mosley puts her finger on what are probably the most important points . . . that the five first volumes of [Williamson's] *Chronicle* are among the very best fictional records of life at the fighting front that we have . . . Ronald Duncan provides a typically combative introduction ("This writer died, cornered by Contemporary cant") and Ted Hughes's contribution is a moving and intelligent funeral address.' *TLS*
Illustrated. 192 pp. Cased. £10.95